AF880270

ANISH
KAPOOR

ANISH KAPOOR

LYNDA FORSHA

with an essay by PIER LUIGI TAZZI

MUSEUM OF CONTEMPORARY ART
SAN DIEGO

This project and publication have been made possible by the National Endowment for the Arts, the Elizabeth W. Russell Foundation, and The British Council; and by generous contributions from Rea and Lela Axline, Charles C. and Sue K. Edwards, Carolyn Farris, Mason and Elizabeth Phelps, Michael Krichman and Leslie Simon, Matthew and Iris Strauss, and Beeba's Creations, Inc.

EXHIBITION ITINERARY

Museum of Contemporary Art, San Diego
February 1 - July 5, 1992

Des Moines Art Center, Des Moines, Iowa
January 30 - April 25, 1993

National Gallery of Canada, Ottawa
July 9 - September 19, 1993

The Power Plant, Toronto
November 1993 - January 1994

ISBN 0-934418-38-1
Library of Congress Number: 91-67707

Front & Back Cover: *UNTITLED* (details), 1991
marble
68 1/2" x 35 1/2 " x 36 1/2"

CONTENTS

FOREWORD

THIS MUSEUM HAS TAKEN great pride in patronizing a succession of leading British sculptors over the past seven years. Offering in most instances their first significant North American exhibitions, we have also provided these artists with support to create new works by means of residencies. Starting with Bill Woodrow's summer stay of 1985, Eric Snell's in 1986, and Richard Long's in 1989, each artist brought family to this seaside resort for a productive few weeks of work and relaxation. In every case the Museum and community benefited by their company, their exhibitions, and the acquisition of significant work for the collection. Additionally, we were pleased to host a modest Tony Cragg exhibition in 1986, and look forward to showing Antony Gormley's work in 1992, as well as to supporting a residency with David Mach in 1993. Thus, our current residency and exhibition with Anish Kapoor continues a San Diego tradition while extending a British trend.

Kapoor's exhibition for the British entry at the most recent Venice Biennale in 1990 was a rare triumph. Stunningly beautiful and spiritually powerful, the sequence of assembled sculpture transformed the feel of the old pavilion from Colonial tea house to Hindu temple. No small feat in the commodity-charged atmosphere of an international art show, but also confirming and salutary evidence of the diversity and strength of culture in Britain at the end of a difficult century.

Amongst Kapoor's powerful sculptural congregation in Venice, one work, *The Healing of St. Thomas*, stood apart for its diminutive size and as the only piece that physically altered the fabric of the exhibition space. Pierced deep into the wall but flush with the surface, this foot-long, lips-shaped, red-pigmented gash embodies the complex sensual and spiritual integration of Kapoor's sensibility. The title alludes to "doubting Thomas," the apostle who thrust his hand into Christ's side before accepting the validity of His resurrected appearance. But the Christian interpretation can be balanced by a Freudian analysis. Just as the piece's content may be sacred and profane, its profile is both geometric and organic and, at first glance, even its status as two-dimensional shape or three-dimensional form is ambiguous. As architectural "intervention," this work signaled a new direction that Kapoor is pursuing with site-specific installations at the hosting venues of the current exhibition. We are proud to have added *The Healing of St. Thomas* to our Museum's permanent collection and we are grateful to the Elizabeth W. Russell Foundation for funding both this significant acquisition and Kapoor's residency in San Diego. We are similarly grateful to our Museum colleagues in this country and in Canada with whom we are sharing this exhibition. Likewise, we are greatly indebted to the institutions and individuals who have supported this endeavor financially.

Finally, Anish Kapoor receives our deepest thanks–his good humor and generosity are only matched by the extraordinary caliber of his great art.

HUGH M. DAVIES
Director

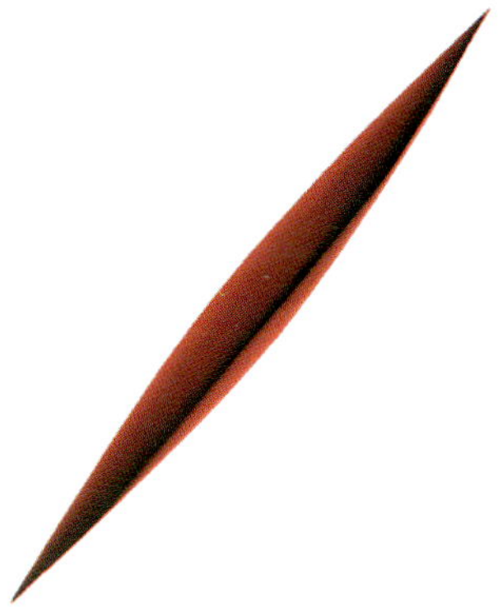

ACKNOWLEDGMENTS

AS THE 1991 RECIPIENT of the prestigious Turner Prize, Anish Kapoor has been recognized as one of the most important artists working today, and we take great pride in having organized the first West Coast exhibition of his work and the first U.S. exhibition to tour in the United States and in Canada. First and foremost we would like to thank those who have contributed so generously to this important project. Without the significant support of the Elizabeth W. Russell Foundation, the National Endowment for the Arts, and The British Council, this exhibition and catalogue would not have been possible. Our sincere thanks also goes to the individuals who have made contributions: Lela and Rea Axline, Sue K. and Charles C. Edwards, Carolyn Farris, Elizabeth and Mason Phelps, Michael Krichman and Leslie Simon, Matthew and Iris Strauss, and to our corporate contributor, Beeba's Creations, Inc. For their support of this project and recognition of its significance we are truly grateful. We also extend our appreciation to the Empress Hotel of La Jolla for graciously hosting Anish Kapoor during his residency.

With the support of the Russell Foundation and its board of directors (Richard Armstrong, Mary Beebe, Hugh Davies, Patrick J. Ledden, Sheldon Nodelman, Patricia Patterson, and Jehanne Teilhet-Fisk), we were able to continue the Museum's Artist-in-Residence program with the Department of Visual Arts at the University of California, San Diego. As 1992 Russell Foundation Artist-in-Residence, Anish Kapoor had the opportunity to work with the department's faculty and students. We thank B.J. Barclay, graduate advisor of the Department of Visual Arts, for her assistance in coordinating Kapoor's time at the university. We are grateful, as always, to Louise Noodleman, business officer for the Russell Foundation, for her indispensable efforts as liaison between the foundation and the Museum.

The interest and involvement of the British government, through a grant from The British Council, is most appreciated, and I would like to acknowledge Gordon Tindale, Cultural Attaché in Washington, D.C., and John Houlton, Vice Consul (Information) in Los Angeles, for their assistance.

As the National Endowment for the Arts contributed a major grant to this project, it seems appropriate to acknowledge here the extraordinary contributions the NEA makes to our nation's arts organizations, ours included. Their support is critical to the realization of important projects such as this, and we are very grateful.

Throughout the organization of this project, the support and efforts of those galleries representing Kapoor's work have been invaluable. Nicholas Logsdail and the staff of the Lisson Gallery, London, especially Bonnie Rubenstein, have graciously responded to countless requests and inquiries. In New York, Barbara Gladstone, Richard Flood, and the staff of the Barbara Gladstone Gallery have assisted in many ways.

Our thanks go to the Rijksmuseum Kröller-Müller in The Netherlands and Marianne Brouwer, Curator, for agreeing to lend *Untitled* from their collection for this exhibition and its international tour.

The organization of this exhibition and publication has involved the support and creative efforts of many individuals on the Museum's staff, to whom I am indebted. For his unflagging interest and support in the realization of this project and for his characteristic enthusiasm from start to finish, I would like to extend my heartfelt thanks to Hugh Davies. Assisting him in securing the needed financial resources were Anne Farrell, and in administering the project, Charles Castle. I am grateful to them as well as to Nerissa Dominguez and Marie Vickers Horne for their dedication and perseverance throughout the organization of the exhibition and its catalogue. They attended to the relentless details associated with compiling the biography and bibliography and coordinating Kapoor's Russell residency with UCSD's Department of Visual Arts. My deep appreciation is extended to Bill Bulkley and Tom Flowers for their patience throughout, as changes were made to the exhibition plans, and for their tenacity and resolve in tackling myriad engineering and installation challenges. All the crating, shipping, and customs arrangements were expertly orchestrated through the skilled and resourceful efforts of Mary Johnson, who also assisted the project in countless ways. Philipp Scholz Rittermann captured the essence of the installation in his photographs for this publication, which was thoughtfully designed by Dennis Sopczynski and edited with insight by Julie Dunn. Others among the staff involved with the success of the exhibition were Suzannah Banet, Liza Boyer, Matthew Clowminzer, Joan Dalrymple, Gretchen Davison, Linda Fonte, Gwen Fowler, Madeleine Grynsztejn, Tauno Hannula, Michelle Hautau, Greg Kahn, Wendy LaBron, Cheryl Butler Lee, Diane Maxwell, Lisa Morrow, Chris Overson, Terry Overson, Debra Palmer, Juanita Purner, Erika Torri, and Ellie Winans.

We owe a special thanks to Jeff Dyson, Anish Kapoor's assistant, who traveled to San Diego for the installation and whose expertise proved invaluable. In London, Andrew Penketh and Tim Shutter were essential to the making of the work. Scot Blyth of MOMART was instrumental in arranging crating and transportation for the exhibition tour, and we are grateful for his good efforts.

Our appreciation also goes out to those who have shared this exhibition with us: I. Michael Danoff, Director, and Jessica Rowe, Associate Director, of the Des Moines Art Center; Shirley Thompson, Director, Catherine Jensen, Acting Chief of Exhibitions, and Diana Nemiroff, Curator of Contemporary Canadian Art, of the National Gallery of Canada in Ottawa; Allan Mackay, Director, and Louise Dompierre, Associate Director and Chief Curator, of The Power Plant in Toronto.

It was Anish Kapoor's wish that we invite Italian writer, poet, and curator Pier Luigi Tazzi to contribute a text for this catalogue. Tazzi's essay doesn't attempt to describe and explain Kapoor's work but rather serves to broaden the cultural boundaries through which Kapoor's work functions. Context and poetic endeavor are revealed and extended in Tazzi's companion text, which was translated with great sensitivity by Marguerite Shore. We are grateful for their contribution to this project.

Finally, it has been a great privilege and a genuine pleasure to work over the past few years with Anish Kapoor, an artist of extraordinary vision, sensitivity and integrity, whose work, intelligence, and friendship have provided me with inspiration throughout.

LYNDA FORSHA
Curator

INTRODUCTION

ENTERING A MUSEUM TODAY, one expects to be confronted, challenged, and cajoled by the work of proactive artists who make the burning issues of our day central to their purpose. This socially and politically charged work appropriately focuses our attention outward and toward a collective consciousness. Yet equally important for human survival is attention focused inward and toward continual nourishment of our spiritual beings. Anish Kapoor reaffirms continuity with the tradition of artist as aesthetician and philosopher, the time-honored practicioner who makes work which is classical in form and universal in content.

Extending the tradition of the "abstract sublime," Kapoor's contemplative work elicits vast areas of human experience and explores the land of the psychological, the spiritual, the metaphysical, and the metaphoric through a vocabulary of archetypal images. The origins of his personal and enigmatic forms may be attributed, in part, to his rich cultural background. Born in Bombay, India, and educated in London, Kapoor's interest in Indian art and mythology and his exposure to a variety of cultural traditions have been essential to the evolution of his themes and artistic vocabulary.

The sensuous pigmented sculptures of Anish Kapoor were exhibited for the first time almost a decade ago. Primal in spirit, these communities of floor-bound forms–architectonic, organic, and sexual in orientation–speak a universal language yet remain aloof, exotic, and mysterious. Pigment dusted on and around each object functions as a shroud and conceals the hand of the artist. As if self-manifest, they appear to be erupting through the floor. These early works brought Kapoor to international attention in the early 1980s, and he has since been recognized as one of the most original British sculptors.

In 1990 Kapoor represented Great Britain at the 44th Venice Biennale, and that exhibition of works from the late 1980s traveled throughout Europe. Focusing on more recent works, our exhibition includes new sculptures made in Kapoor's London studio as well as installations created by the artist for each institution. Visits to the museums participating in the tour and subsequent residencies allowed the artist to make works specific to the distinct character of each site. Trips to San Diego in 1990 and 1991 resulted in three new installations. *When I Am Pregnant*, a subtle yet perceptually complex wall installation, has been made for the Gordon Gray Lobby; *The Earth*, a floor excavation, transforms the space of the large West Gallery; and *Endless Column*, a red-pigmented floor-to-ceiling shaft, penetrates and activates the space of the Meyer Gallery. These installation works are juxtaposed with sculptures made of sandstone, marble, slate and fiberglas, chosen and installed to underscore themes and relationships characteristic of his current work.

With these recent sculptures, Kapoor is looking inward. The exhibition clearly reveals a shift in interest from the exterior surfaces of objects to their dematerialized interiors, and from monolithic objects to site-specific installations that physically intervene and transform the architectural space. Central to this venture is the demonstration of sculptor Kapoor exploring the Renaissance convention of painting as illusionistic window or space beyond, while never deviating from his commitment to work that is wholly sculptural and very much physically present. His focus on interiority is especially evident in sculptures and installations that suggest or actually provide glimpses into deep, pigmented, and impenetrable spaces. The metaphoric power of these womblike inner realms is generated as the viewer is visually and viscerally drawn into the work. Instead of relying on unitary interpretations for his works, Kapoor allows the viewer to experience his or her own personal contemplative and spiritual nature. The darkness inherent in the recent work reflects Kapoor's current preoccupation with what he describes in his own words as "images of dark and dangerous dieties, seen as they emerge from a potent subconscious world, some essential element from the dark side of the human psyche."[1] For Kapoor this interior world is made up of forces which play against each other, either in opposition or striving for union. Basic dualities exist within individual works and between works: earth/sky, masculine/feminine, form/formlessness, presence/absence. These primal juxtapositions are fundamental to Kapoor's desire for unity through the fusion of opposing forces, and in this exhibition one becomes sensitized to the sculptor's quiet intention of guiding the viewer through a perceptual narrative, a deliberate but subtle progression of phenomenological sculptural experiences.

The first work encountered in the Museum's entry gallery, *When I Am Pregnant*, is a voluptuous swollen wall suggestive of growth, fecundity, and the creative process. It appears mysteriously and simultaneously both present and absent. Viewed from the side, the volumetric form bulges twelve inches from the wall, yet from the front it dematerializes into whiteness and optically fluctuates between concave and convex form. In making the work, Kapoor recalled a story of Japanese Zen monks exchanging the greeting, "Are you pregnant yet?" The idea of being not just physically full but spiritually complete is the subject of this work and takes us beyond the realm of the formal and perceptual to a more philosophical plane.

Perhaps the most phenomenologically arresting installation in the exhibition is *The Earth*, a work which reads as a black circle painted on the floor but is, in fact, a hole cut through the floor. Approximately two feet in diameter, this negative space appears to have indeterminate depth and draws one like a magnet to peer into a seemingly bottomless pit. The physicality and presence of *The Earth* is extraordinary and undeniable, and at the same time perplexing, considering it is no more than a negative space, a sculptural presence that is nonphysical. Kapoor has made something out of nothing; the more non-existent his forms become, the richer the experience they provide.

Installed in an apselike configuration where two large, half-spherical, wall-mounted forms face each other and the third faces out, *Untitled* is seen as the viewer completes the quadrant while enveloped in this chapel of perceptual reverie. Painted Prussian blue inside and out, the forms absorb light within and give no pespectival clues to their seemingly impenetrable interior depth. One peers into the realm beyond—of darkness, the heavens, and the vast space of our own internal world. Kapoor's primary concern is creating illusory negative space within these forms he describes as "voids." "The more I leave myself out, the easier it is for the work to have a life of its own. The more I empty out, the more there is. Emptying out is filling up."[2]

Angel, a work that comprises eight large slate slabs unaltered in any way except by the saturated application of more than a dozen coats of Prussian blue pigment, seems to float in space. Randomly placed, these ponderous stones are visually contradicted by their weightless appearance and suggest the transformation of slabs of earth into chunks of sky. Kapoor describes this process in almost alchemical terms: "If art is about anything, then it's about transformation. It is about changing one state of matter into another. And that happens not by willing it to change, but by some strange process of manipulation which I wouldn't know how to talk about. I am sure if I were to insist that these forms were quarried blocks of Prussian blue, you'd believe me."[3]

Of the three new stone sculptures made for the exhibition, the two sandstone works are the most conspicuously related to Kapoor's on-site installations. The interiors of both trapezoidal blocks of sandstone have been hollowed out from one side revealing physical presences within. A column form in *Pillar of Light* directly relates to his installation *Endless Column*, and *The Presence of Form* echoes the bulge in *When I Am Pregnant*. Like an even shaft of light piercing through, the column form in *Pillar of Light* is in contrast to the darkness behind, as its title describes. The excavated fronts of these massive forms are slightly below eye level, encouraging the viewer to stoop a bit to see into their protected and carefully chiseled interiors. In looking at traditional Indian art, Kapoor has made discoveries about the way in which spirit has been embodied in interior space. "I'm thinking of the kind of space that there might be in an image of a meditating Buddha, where all attention is focused inward."[4] This figurative sculpture described by Kapoor has underlying it an abstract, mental language, a condition Kapoor is working towards in making his own art.

Embodying his aesthetic of fundamental duality and his predilection for frontal orientation, the absolutely smooth plane on the face of *Untitled* is countered by an irregular and rough surface on all other sides. An ovoid shape seems to float on the front of the work and fluctuates between organic and geometric, slowly revealing an interior realm. Its human scale belies the multi-ton weight of milky white Carerra marble, and the proportions of this rectangular slab of marble found by Kapoor in a stone yard in Northern England seemed ideal, as though quarried for a figurative work. With as little intervention as possible on the exterior surface, Kapoor chose to core out an egg-shaped form as though revealing the womb. We are given access to a secret interior space, a protected inner sanctuary, a place of repose, a room without corners. The womb, suggested and exteriorized in *When I Am Pregnant*, has been turned inside out.

Thrusting through the otherwise empty gallery from floor to ceiling, Kapoor's *Endless Column* seems the positive counterpart to *The Earth*. Blood-red pigment has been applied to the surface of this eighteen-inch-diameter shaft, and additional pigment extends outward, daubed on in circles, floor and ceiling, furthering the illusion of penetration beneath and above the room and recalling Kapoor's early pigmented work. The most assertive work in the exhibition, *Endless Column* seems the male equivalent to Brancusi's repeating tight-waisted female forms.

An artist of enormous facility and range, Kapoor's achievements synthesize the formal concerns of Post-Minimalist sculpture with an Eastern spiritual sensibility as he explores the relationship between physicality and transcendence. In sum, the exhibition he has created is much more than its constituent parts. There are nine discrete works in the exhibition, and a tenth could be considered the conjunction of all the pieces. In spite of the seemingly opposing characteristics of his forms, there remains a consistency and coherency of ideas. Where there is light, we turn a corner and find darkness; one room is full, the next empty; where there is weight in one area, there is weightlessness in another. Solid/void, interior/exterior, body/spirit are played against each other and are expressed by the artist in subtle and sometimes astonishing ways. References to the body abound, from the humanness of scale to the use of blood-red pigment. Wounds, orifices and places within–both sacred and taboo–are carved out, providing access to the world of the subconscious.

> *I think there are basically two kinds of artists: those who look to reveal the wound–the wound that we all carry–and then there are artists who look within their own methodology to redemption toward the healing of that wound. I am clearly of the second kind.* [5]

LYNDA FORSHA
Curator

1. Connie Lewallen, "Interview with Anish Kapoor, Japan, September, 1990," *View* (San Francisco: Crown Point Press, Fall 1991), 16.

2. Lynda Forsha, interview with Anish Kapoor, Museum of Contemporary Art, San Diego, February 2, 1992.

3. Ibid.

4. Ibid.

5. Ibid.

BREATH OF AIR, BREATH OF STONE

A HORIZONTAL VECTOR, the recognition/drawing of a direction, moves in rapid acceleration. But there are obstacles, abysses, chasms of emptiness, oases of inactivity, pockets of retention, rapid whirlpools and outflows that drag everything into an indefinable elsewhere. And yet the drawing of the vector, of the vectorial line, becomes increasingly precise, more defined, more taut, more cutting.

Where does this vectorial line come from and where is it going? Where does one find its point of departure? Where is its end point, its destiny?

Let us, for a moment, take Renaissance perspective as a model, which, for better or worse, still remains the most perfect model (we know that "the most perfect" does not exist—nothing is beyond the perfect, beyond perfection, perfection implies the end of a process). And let's call it the most complete model that Western culture has achieved, but which is also its point of origin, its incunabulum, its original "form."[1] I am expanding the use of the term "perspective" beyond its own disciplinary limits, to use it as a model of culture. And that expansion is fundamental, for within a particular era, within the sphere of a particular culture, a system of representation has become a model of culture: vision has come to be privileged, to acquire a primacy over the other senses that constitute the human aesthesis. A type of production that immediately responds to vision will have to correspond, consequently, to the primacy accorded vision, and this will be the image. The production of images will have to take advantage of the most precise possible mechanism, to reconstruct the object of vision. This is less a question of "truth" than one of efficaciousness, of effect.

Brunelleschi's second panel, described by Antonio Manetti in his *Vita di Filippo Brunelleschi*,[2] represents the Palazzo dei Signori—today called the Palazzo Vecchio; it is accurately cut out of the upper edge, where the profile of the buildings was delineated against the sky (today one would say skyline). If one were to take the panel to the place where it was drawn (a certain corner of the Piazza dei Signori—today called the Piazza della Signoria—in Florence), it would be evident that from one point, and from one point only, the painted image superimposes the natural view with precise exactitude (in any case with one eye closed and with an immobile glance). In this way one would have a very broad approximation of an analogy between the constructed image and the visual perception of the place represented. Brunelleschi's panel is neither a mechanical marvel nor a work of art: it is a tool, useful less for the perception of reality than for the reduction of the aesthetic-cognitive experience (enjoyment of the view, knowledge of the appearance of the piazza and the palazzo, seen from a precise point) to an image. The result is an enormous saving of energy: a complex experience of total aesthesis is replaced by the visual perception of an image; a transferable object/sign is constructed, in opposition to the irremovability of the object of vision; the pertinence of the image/sign is revealed in relation with the space/event, as is, consequently, the efficacious practice of this sort of operation.

And so the model of perspective is this: the reduction of complexity in order to achieve greater comprehension, the construction of simulacra, which are pertinent to the degree that, through them, one can control, dominate, and know the object of simulation, favoring function over substance.

Located this side of perspective, on the side of the subject, there is an area that is indistinct, because it is not an object of representation. This is not the place that is observed but the place occupied by the observer, the place from which vision begins and is generated. This is the starting point, which later can be left out of consideration, ignored, forgotten, treated as if it didn't exist, but not annihilated, for it is there, and it remains, dense and inscrutable, charged. In contrast, vision which has its origin here is light, aerial, transparent, and extends, piercing the space as far as infinity, reaching an area where it becomes less distinct, and even beyond, in that ultimate void beyond appearance. It is clear that there will be obstacles, limits, impasses, and yet the supporting power of vision, its essence, consists of that materiality. As vision encounters things in the world, those things react or set up a resistance; in any case, vision passes through them, and they, by their oppositional nature, become a measure of two aspects: effects and appearances.

If a work, if the work of an artist, of this artist, of Anish Kapoor, participates in these two realities, if it is located at this crest, at this point of distinction, one has to wonder how and at what moment, in what place, from what point of view (but where then is the point of view?), from what inclination it will be observable. Will it have to be observed in the same way that one observes the still, congealed image of vision? Or will we encounter it along our own path, which has barely diverged from what is understood as a principal axis?

I am visiting some artists in Zurich. They agree to meet for an interview at a café. When we meet there, one of them says to me, by way of justification: "Excuse us for not inviting you to the studio. But, as you know, all artists' studios are the same: the tools of the trade, some projects roughed out, a bit of paint, some left over dirt." And this is the reality in most cases. But not always. Not always. Sometimes these places are exquisite, unique in a way that is absolute. Not so much because they bear the traces of the artist's work, that is, because they are the artist's laboratory, workshop, tool, and totality of tools and materials from which the work will spring forth, the terrain that will sprout the work, which will then be settled into galleries. And even less because the studio reflects the artist's personality, the lair, the animal-man's nest, the closed room, the driver's cab equipped for a voyage in the world. Both such cases would be versions, variants of the laboratory or the dwelling place. The studio is something else: the place of the work. Not of its birth, not of its author, but its place. Outside that place, the work will be something else: an offshoot, a fragment, a splinter, a thread, a particle, an effect, a result, a projection, a crystallization of this something that has its unity only there; all the rest is insignificant.

And each studio I know is different, not because of what it contains—in fact it contains nothing—but because of what it is.

It is strange, the fate that these places will come up against. There are the ones that I know or those that have vanished (like the studio of Remo Salvadori in Milan or that of Ettore Spalletti in Cappelle sul Tavo in Abruzzi), or those that are about to disappear (like the studio of Herbert Brandl in Vienna or that of Reinhard Mucha in Düsseldorf). It is almost as if they were living creatures that share with every living being the fate of extinction.

And yet the studio is not the site of the creation, but the world after the creation, where man-god has both elected and built, shaped his own dwelling place. It indicates a complexity that transcends the birth of the work in that it is fundamental to creation, it is creation lived by that which is created and that which contains it. Its limits are not those protective ones of the house, but the sacred ones of the temple. But the sacred quality of the space, of this space, is inaccessible. It doesn't open up to any ritual. It is limited to being. It is neither architecture nor construction: it is emanation and expansion to the limits of consciousness, it is the monad irradiated (with or without window).

In the case of Kapoor, the studio is presented as a valley of temples, as a landscape and accumulation of sacred places; it has a polytheistic multiplication, the elements of which are made up of works of art.

Kapoor's studio stands in contrast—to the centralizing and centripetal studio of Mucha, which creates the void that aspires, attracting the dense mass of its own being, the germinal and germinating ovum, fertilized by history; to the expanded and centrifugal studio of Spalletti, which is squeezed against the walls and includes landscape and the color of the sky, and is maternal womb, uterine walls; to the inner life as outer life (nature and culture, body and nourishment) of Brandl (no longer emerging); to the richness of signs and forms, on the scale of Salvadori's worlds (I no longer go out, every exit is in vain if it doesn't lead back to an interior).

Kapoor multiplies the sacred, and this proliferation generates a thousand names. Where one barely distinguishes the old from the new, the born from the unborn, the crude from the refined, the different realities add up and are juxtaposed, each time creating new designs and new horizons of presence and of memory.

In the end, the amputation provoked by the perspectival choice results in something that is anything but painless. The attempt to heal the wound (the cure attempted by Luther through religion is perhaps the most consistent among the oldest ones) is revealed to be worse than evil (so much so that Calvin's God returns to the source of that choice and confirms it).

The pain of the amputation seems to be compensated theoretically by the will to power, but in the end finds comfort (but one knows that we are dealing with a placebo) only in the masochism of sublimation. Western culture and artistic culture, in particular, and with particular specificity, as expression, as declaration of what is intended and felt, assume this character, which becomes distinctive in comparison to other cultures, from other places and other times. If some cultures tend more to fullness (everything is) or conversely to emptiness (nothing is), and not infrequently these extremes end up verging on each other, Western culture, our current culture, is burdened with some sense of loss or lack. This is present in other cultures, or in any case, in the majority of those that I know something about, but in those others, the sense of loss tends to be exorcised and in the end conquered. In our own culture the most we can hope for is a sort of repression, analogous to the phenomenon that psycho-analysis deals with. In the first phase of the modern era (from the Renaissance to the first industrial revolution, but the period apparently unravels beyond these conventional limits), this sentiment was expressed in the grandiose and cosmic drama of a society that thought of itself as universal: from the high of Michelangelo to the low of Caravaggio, with Rembrandt as another, middle ground). And if this was true for art, it was also true for other expressions of the poetic universe, although during this first period, art was the primary expression.

In the subsequent period, which we are still experiencing, the cosmic and collective drama of the first phase is replaced by individual histories and stories, the result of a further separation. There is no longer an organized collective response on the part of the species. Instead it is the individual, separate and divided (the division of labor which results in alienation), who responds responsibly and for all. As the perspectival process develops, it not only fails to reconstruct the amputated body, but, through analysis, the distinction that divides and cuts, it reduces that body to fragments. To reacquire, if only symbolically, the lost unity, beginning with the fragment (and without forgetting analogies that exist between fragment and individual), one resorts to narration.

In modern culture, the narrator holds the position of one who tells of a laceration, a separation, a lack, a loss, of which he or she is simultaneously the creator and the victim. Through the telling, grief and defeat are sublimated. Miss Quested/Forster unknowingly desires the assault of the other in the cave of Marabar, and his/her unconsciousness makes the desire all the more strong. Miss Quested, a character in a novel, accepts the innocent's being called to judgment, being found guilty, she accepts the process that her own action has provoked, and once the punitive machine through which the will to power is expressed has been set in motion, she then obstructs the consequences with the heroic and holy (masochistic) act of her own self-criticism. Forster recounts desire, crime, guilt, as things move along unhappily in a direction they should not have gone. Masochism itself is absolved in the tale, as it is realized in the humiliation of the telling.

If narration as the expression of masochism (declaration of one's own guilt that has no redemption, the recognition of the state of unhappiness as consubstantial to existence and its inevitability) is presented as a primary "poetic" model, it is because there is an assumption of the existence of a positive nature, of an innocence, of a happiness, only glimpsed through unexpected glimmers and hypothesized as the substantial reality of the other.

Anish Kapoor's work is situated in the gap opened up by this hypothesis. Indeed, his work is an instantaneous and emphatic proposition of the other, but it is realized only within the schemes that this culture postulates and upon which it insists.

To quote Pirandello, Kapoor's offering seems to say, "I am she who is believed to be," or even better, it is the uncertain reflection that is sometimes created on the walls of the caves of Marabar:

> *They are dark caves. Even when they open towards the sun, very little light penetrates down the entrance tunnel into the circular chamber. There is little to see, and no eye to see it, until the visitor arrives for his five minutes, and strikes a match. Immediately another flame rises in the depths of the rock and moves toward the surface like an imprisoned spirit; the walls of the circular chamber have been most marvellously polished. The two flames approach and strive to unite, but cannot, because one of them breathes air, the other stone. A mirror inlaid with lovely colours divides the lovers, delicate starts of pink and gray interpose exquisite nebulae, shadings fainter than the tail of a comet or the midday moon, of the evanescent life of the granite, only here visible.*[3]

Kapoor's work is less the offering of the self, the ostentation, of levels of happiness, innocence, positivity, than it is the indication, articulated in phrases, of a truth that encompasses and transcends those levels. Kapoor the artist passes through the masochism of culture, he pierces it and goes on to occupy that place where the masochistic apparatus assumes it can absolve its own ends.

He says: I am that other that you want me to be, I am beauty and truth, since your desire for beauty and truth has enabled me to respond in this way, so that you have looked for no other way, have aspired to no other way. You have not looked at my differently articulated substance, and I "create" the wonder and the terror that you desire. My trick, the staging, is situated beyond the threshold that you have prepared and that you will know how to recognize, and that which you will find beyond the threshold is there for you and for you alone.

An entrance was necessary, so mankind made one. But elsewhere, deeper in the granite, are there certain chambers that have no entrances? Chambers never unsealed since the arrival of the gods? Local report declares that these exceed in number those that can be visited, as the dead exceed the living—four hundred of them, four thousand or million. Nothing is inside them, they were sealed up before the creation of pestilence or treasure; if mankind grew curious and excavated, nothing, nothing would be added to the sum of good or evil.[4]

The conquering of the masochistic threshold is the fact of the work's existence. The work is not the narration of lack and of loss, it doesn't deal with suffering and humiliation, but it is their background, radiant and happy, terrible and empty.

In the end the act is blasphemous, for in the end it reduces the absolute toward which it tends, and which it produces, to the circumstance of a desire, which defines it as being other-than-self and unattainable, and for which, finally, only this aspect of unattainability matters.

Kapoor's absolute remains clad in its sacred garb; the absolute is the sacred, but you will appreciate the sacred only in its profane appearance. Again, he says: This is what your masochism wants, this is what it requires. That which exceeds this request doesn't pertain to you, and the extent to which my work participates and is corroborated, the source from which it draws as from an extremely deep, bottomless well, has nothing to do with your unrequited desire, with your basic masochism, with your unhappiness and what lies beyond it. And yet your unhappiness, the song in which it is expressed, the voice, the tale in which it is narrated, is such only because it is inscribed against that background and circumscribes that background, which I represent because this is what you want of me.

Summer 1982 Venice
The afternoon heat on the lagoon invites lazy excursions. The surfaces of water or of stone appear like unmarked spaces; this is not the best hour for passing through them, for they hold a blinding light. It is the panic hour of loss, the hour of the opening in the light made diaphanous by the rising haze, in the dense air warped by the heat. Every encounter is a relief, every breeze a gift, every area of shadow a refuge. It is that pause in the day that, in this city, precedes the phantasmagoria of evening and of night, which follows the sparkling fatigue of morning. I entered the dockyard to greet a friend who is waiting for me. A friend finely attuned to the skies of Tuscany, those skies as real as the painted ones, which he sees and recognizes equally from the top of the round hill where he was born and where he returns, now with increasing frequency, interrupting a voluntary exile.

We walked together, brushing past a space where an artist was finishing his work. We stopped to look. The flash of a glance. The unexpected kindling and blaze of the few and pure colors stood out like sound tones that emanate from instruments, which, while clearly defined, don't enter the usual and expected typology, and yet which, even in their unusual aspect, we recognized.

The space, which should have been shadowy, was steeped in a clear light, like the opaque whiteness of a soft linen, or the plaster in certain interiors in countries where there is blinding sun. My companion said, "It is Kapoor," and after a brief pause, we moved on. We didn't see other work that afternoon, he didn't mention other names. And, looking back on that afternoon, I don't recall any others.

Another friend during that same period, to whom I could not help but mention that fortuitous encounter, talked to me of the devilish and delighted artist, carefully taking care of things (as he expressed it), like a little demon intent upon constructing and arranging his traps. But perhaps he only wanted to tell me about the beauty that characterizes the demon of seduction, knowing all too well that for me the seduction of beauty is simply irresistible. And what else is there?

PIER LUIGI TAZZI

Translated from Italian by Marguerite Shore.

1. For the meaning of "form," which is thus set off in quotes, see the concept of "symbolic form" in Panofsky (Erwin Panofsky, "Die Perspektive als 'Symbolische Form'" in *Vorträge der Bibliothek Warburg, Vorträge 1924-1925*, Lepzig Berlin, 1927). Also see an earlier definition in Cassirer (Ernst Cassirer, *Philosophie der symbolischen formen*, Leipzig, 1923-25). For perspective as a model of culture and its origins, see Hubert Damisch, "L''orgins' de la perspective" in *Macula* 5/6, 1979, and Pier Luigi Tazzi, "Esterno in un interno: le tavolette brunelleschiane e la fotografia" in *Quaderni Di*, 9, 1989.

2. Antonio di Tuccio Manetti, *Vita di Filippo Brunelleschi*, Milan, 1976.

3. E.M. Forster, *A Passage to India*, 6th ed., Harmondsworth, 1989, p. 138.

4. Ibid., p. 139.

WHEN I AM PREGNANT

WHEN I AM PREGNANT

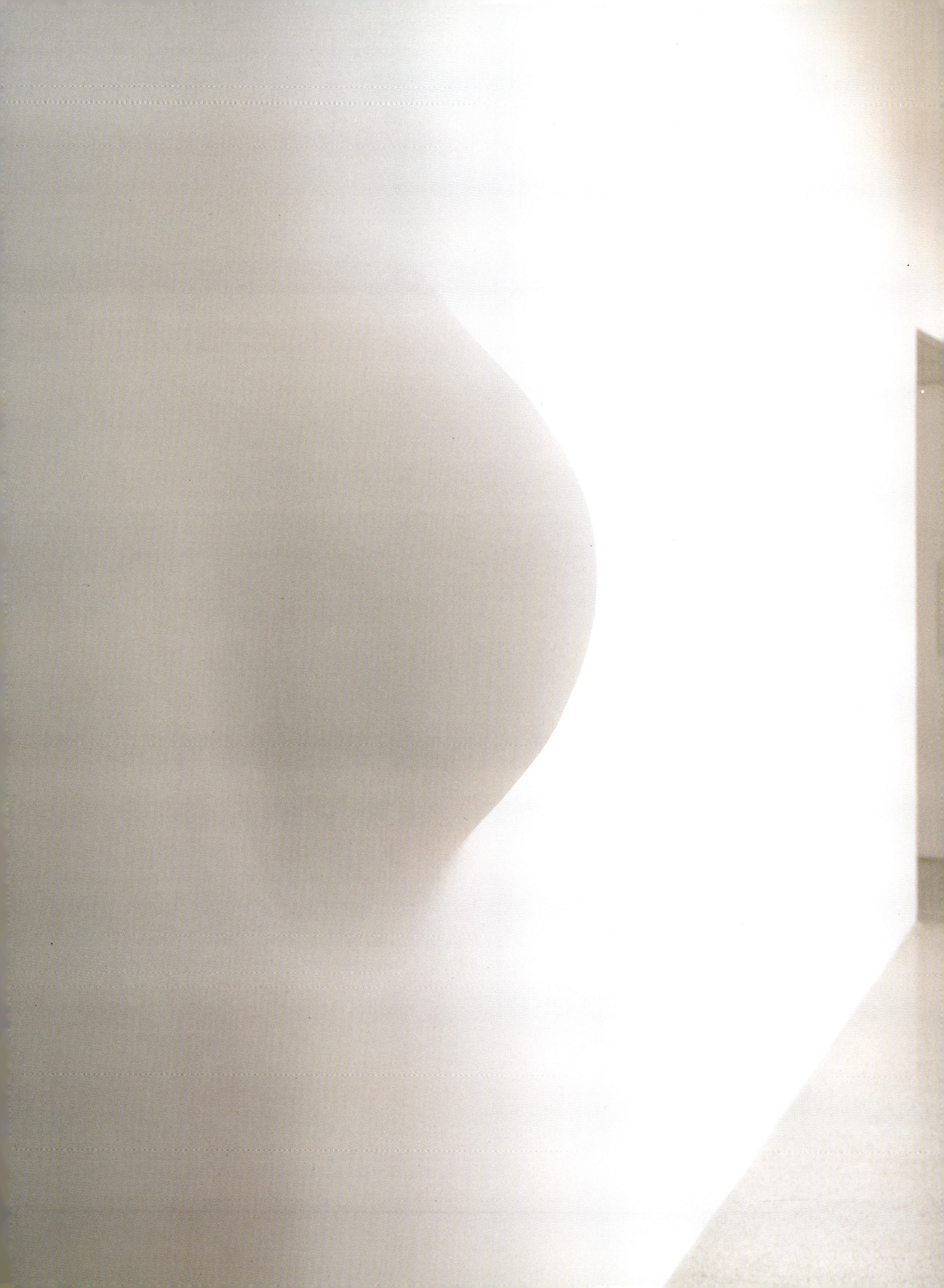

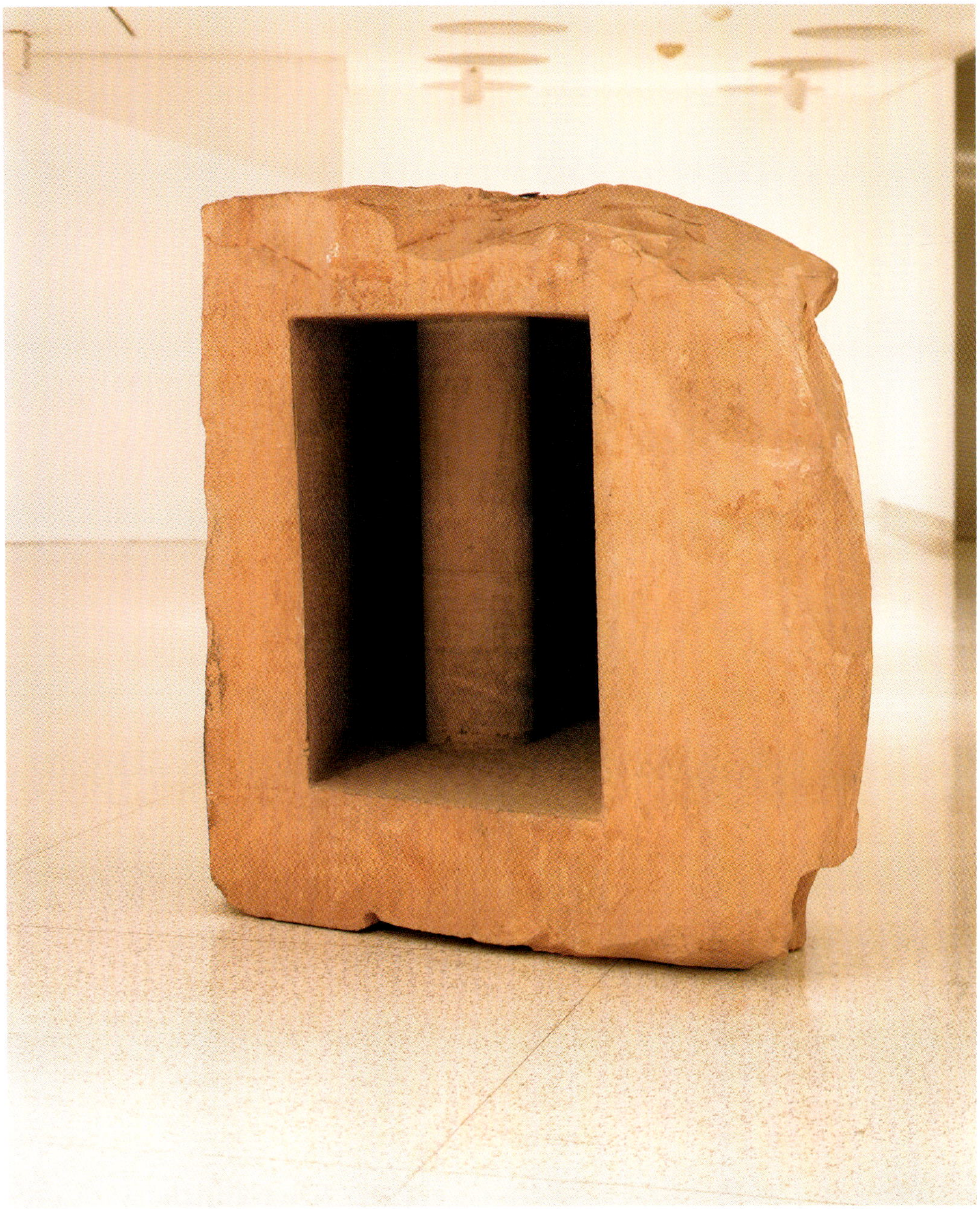

THE HEALING OF ST. THOMAS

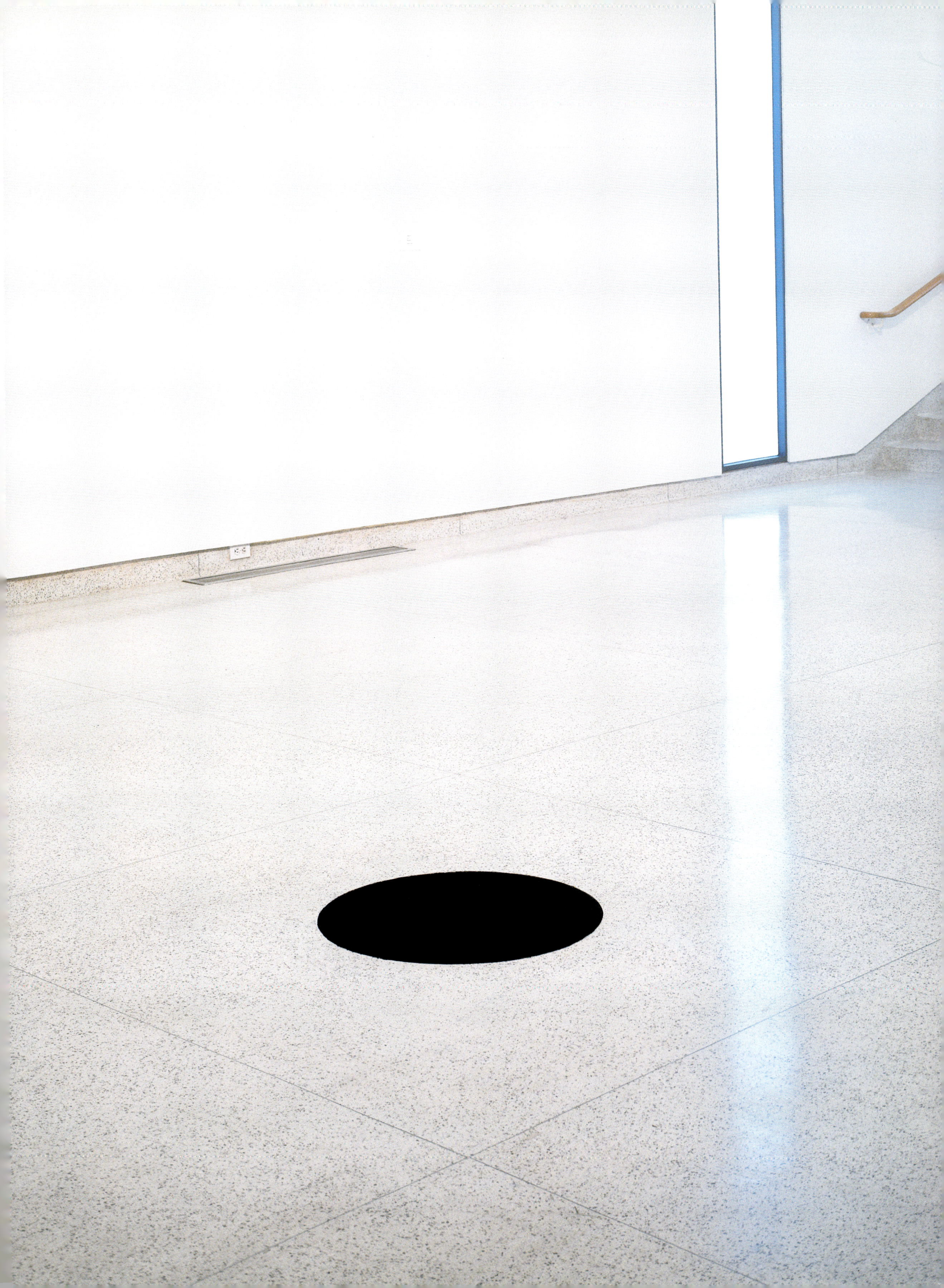

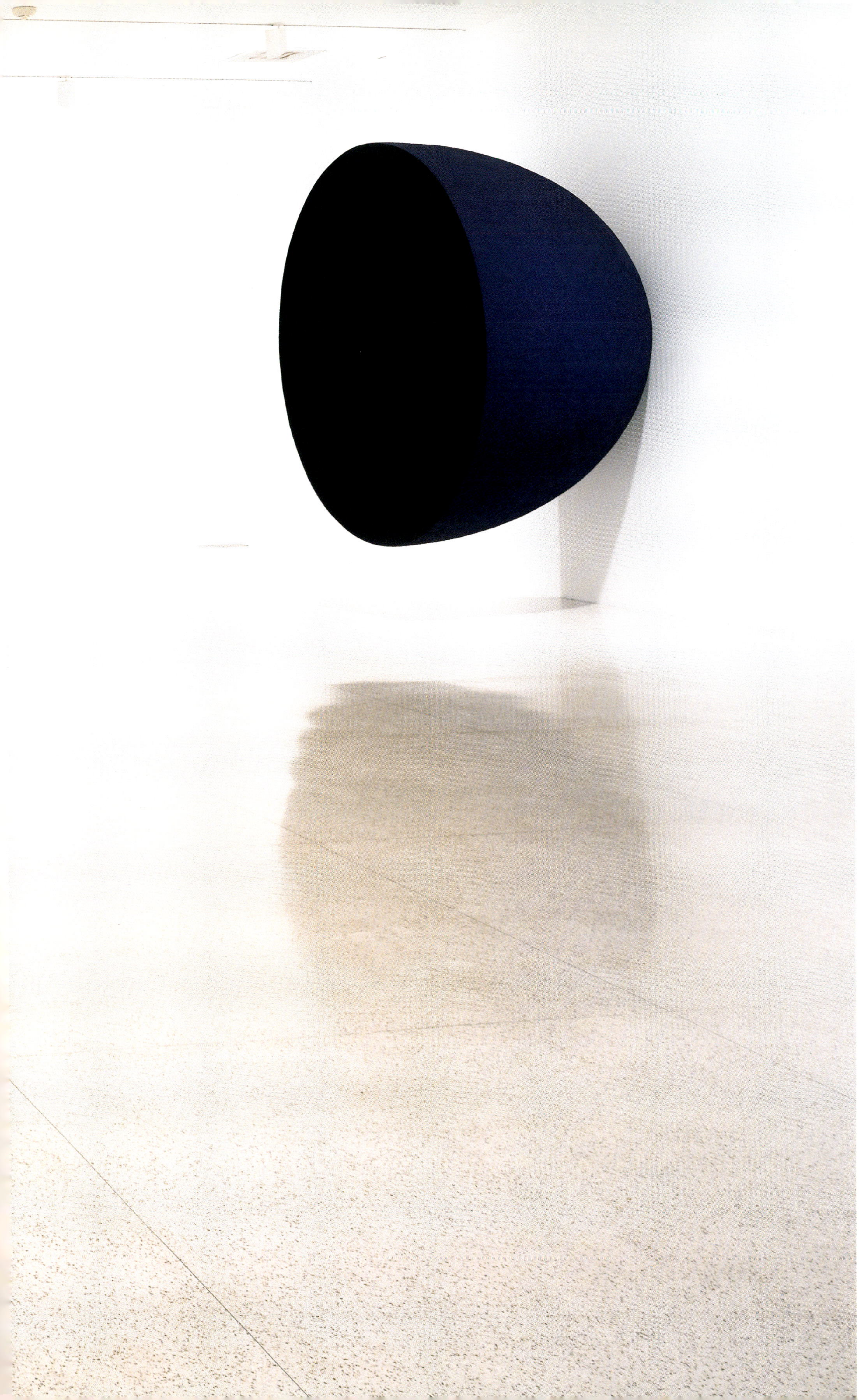

UNTITLED

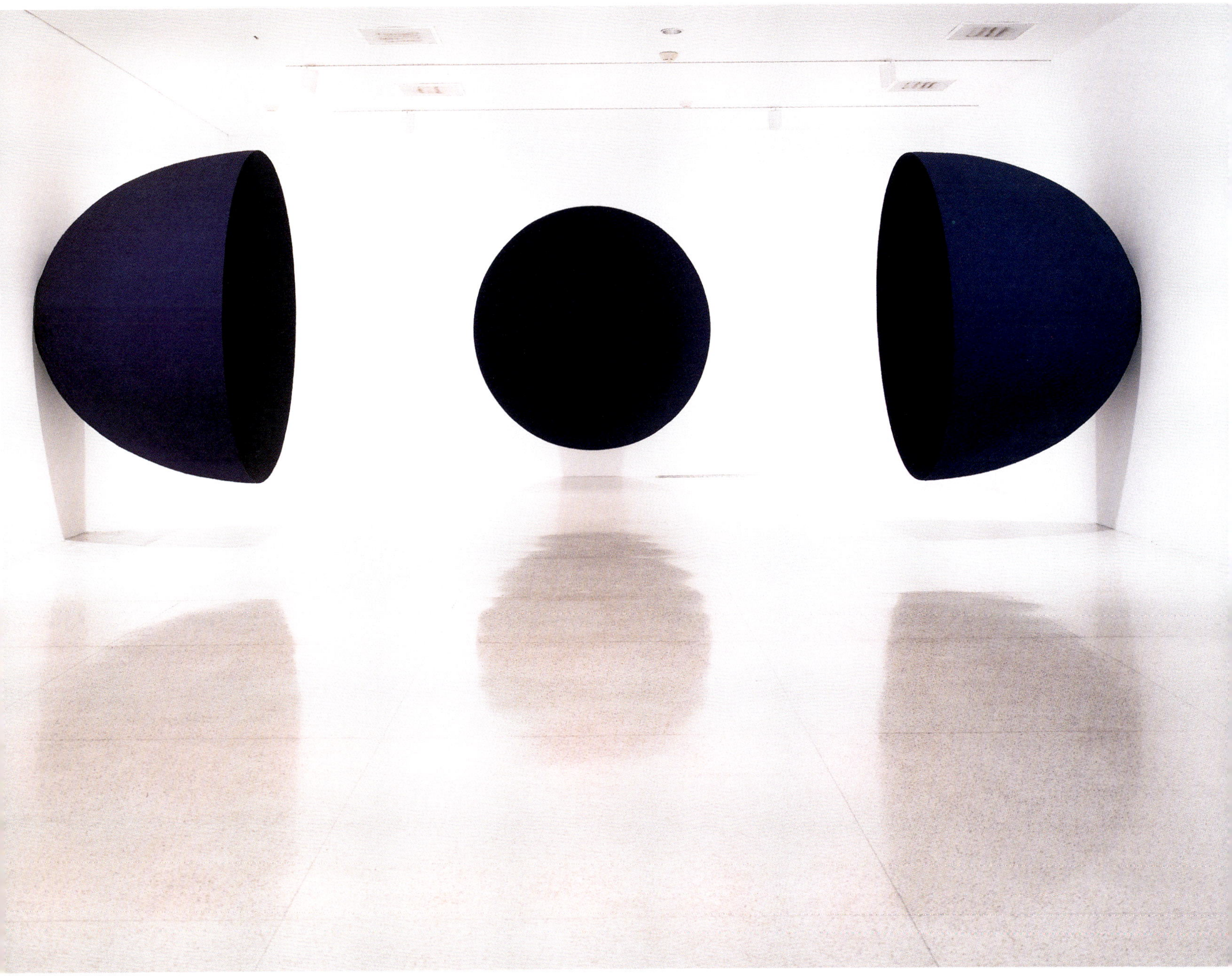

ANGEL

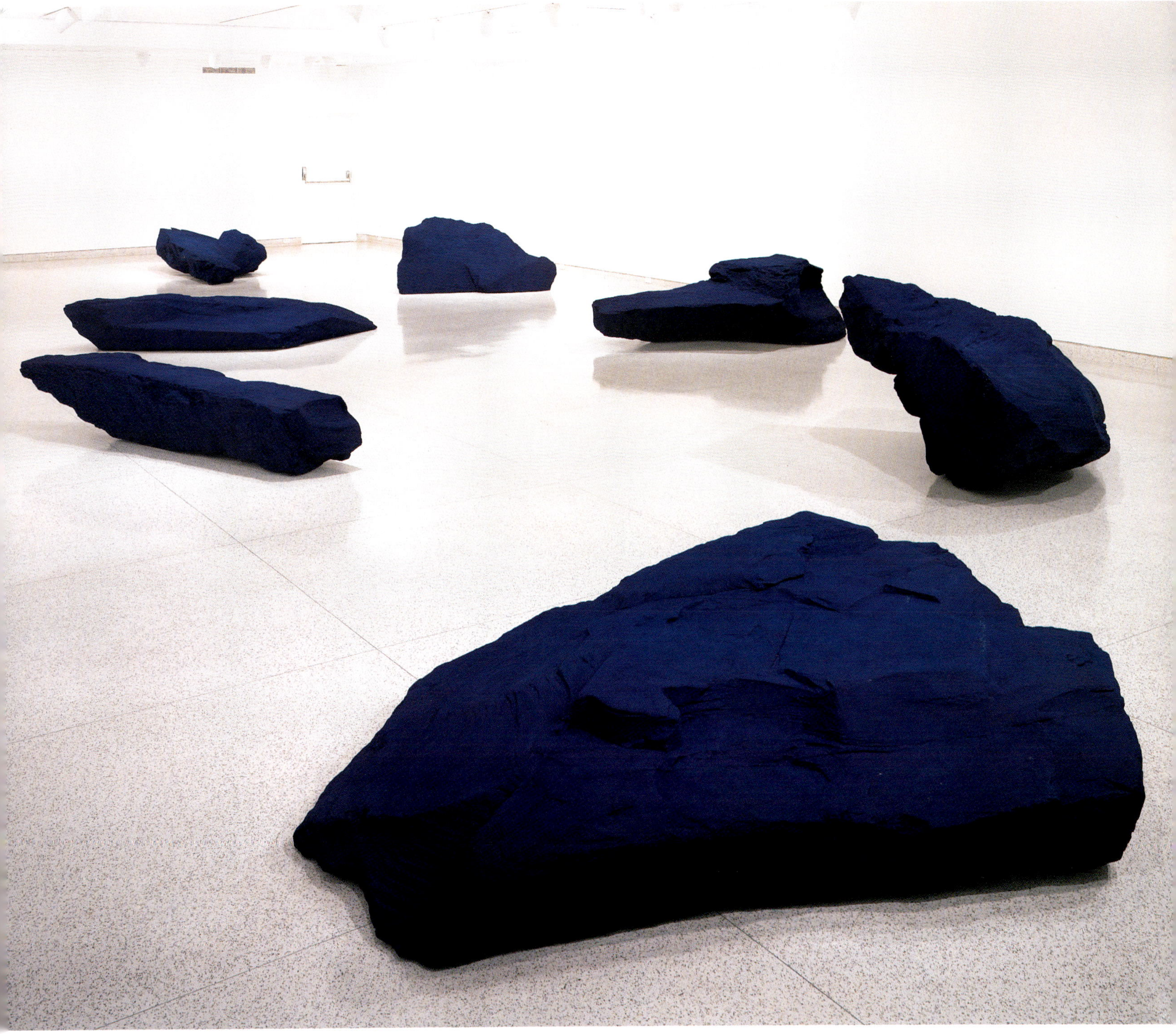

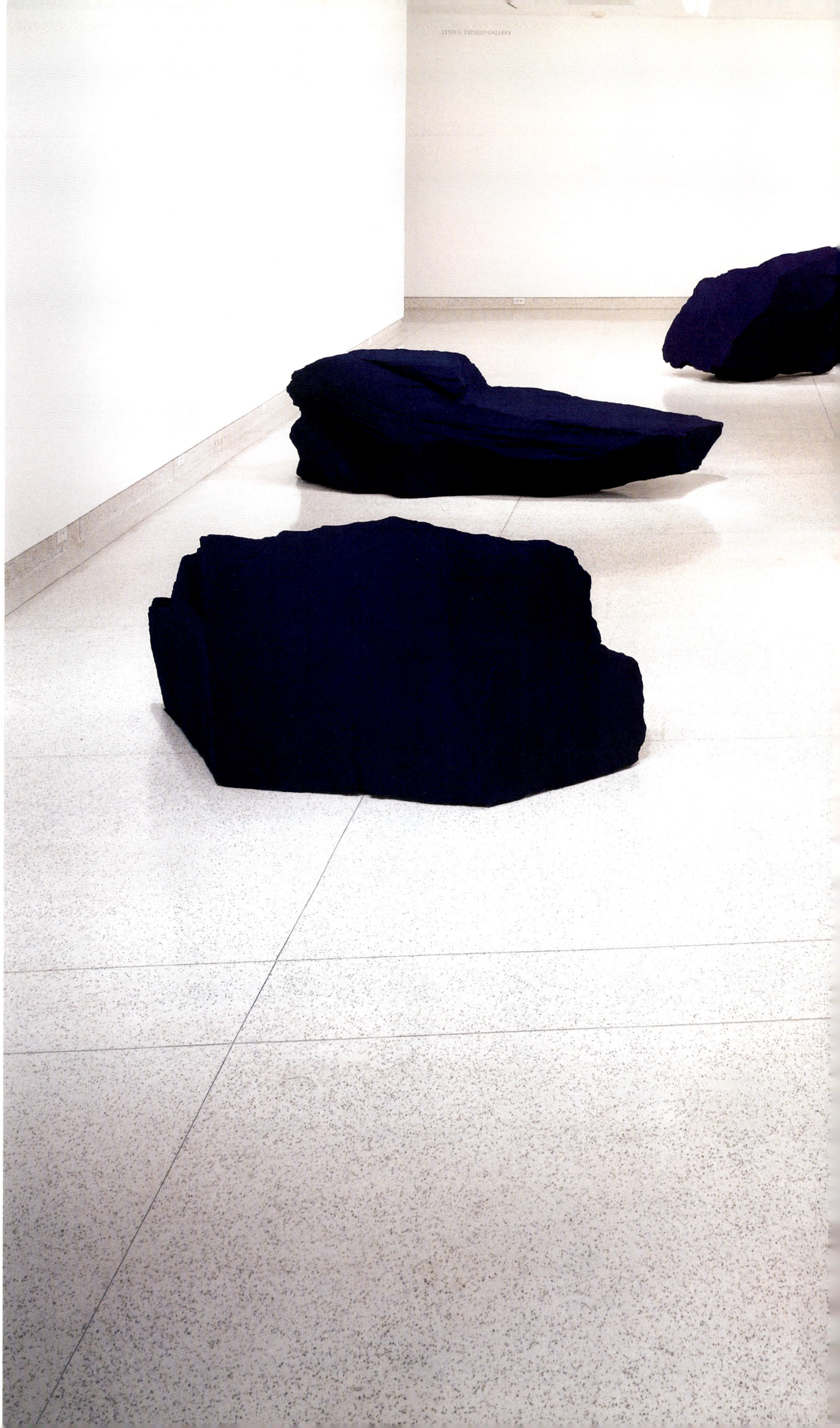
LYNN G. PAYMAN GALLERY

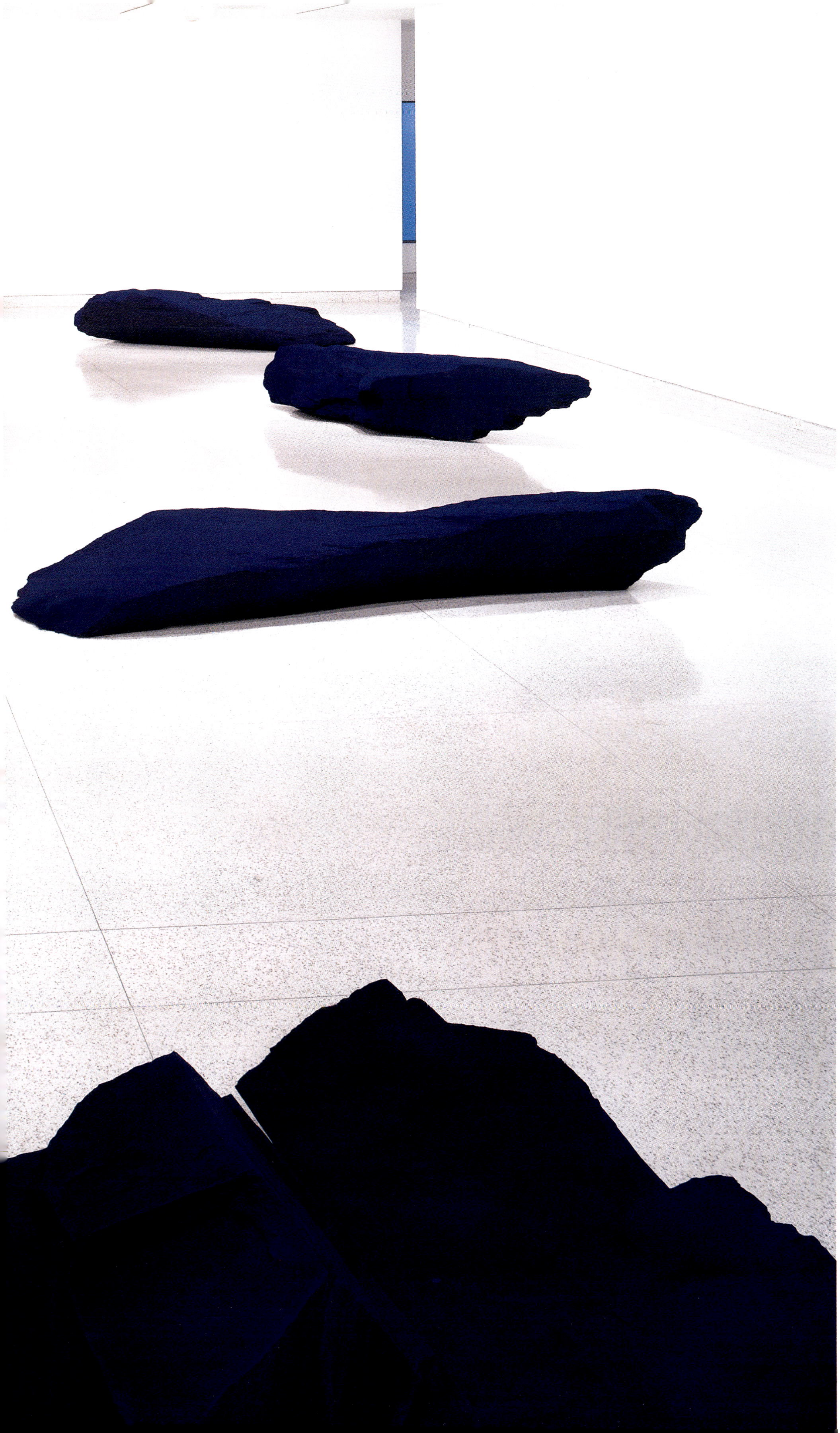

ANGEL

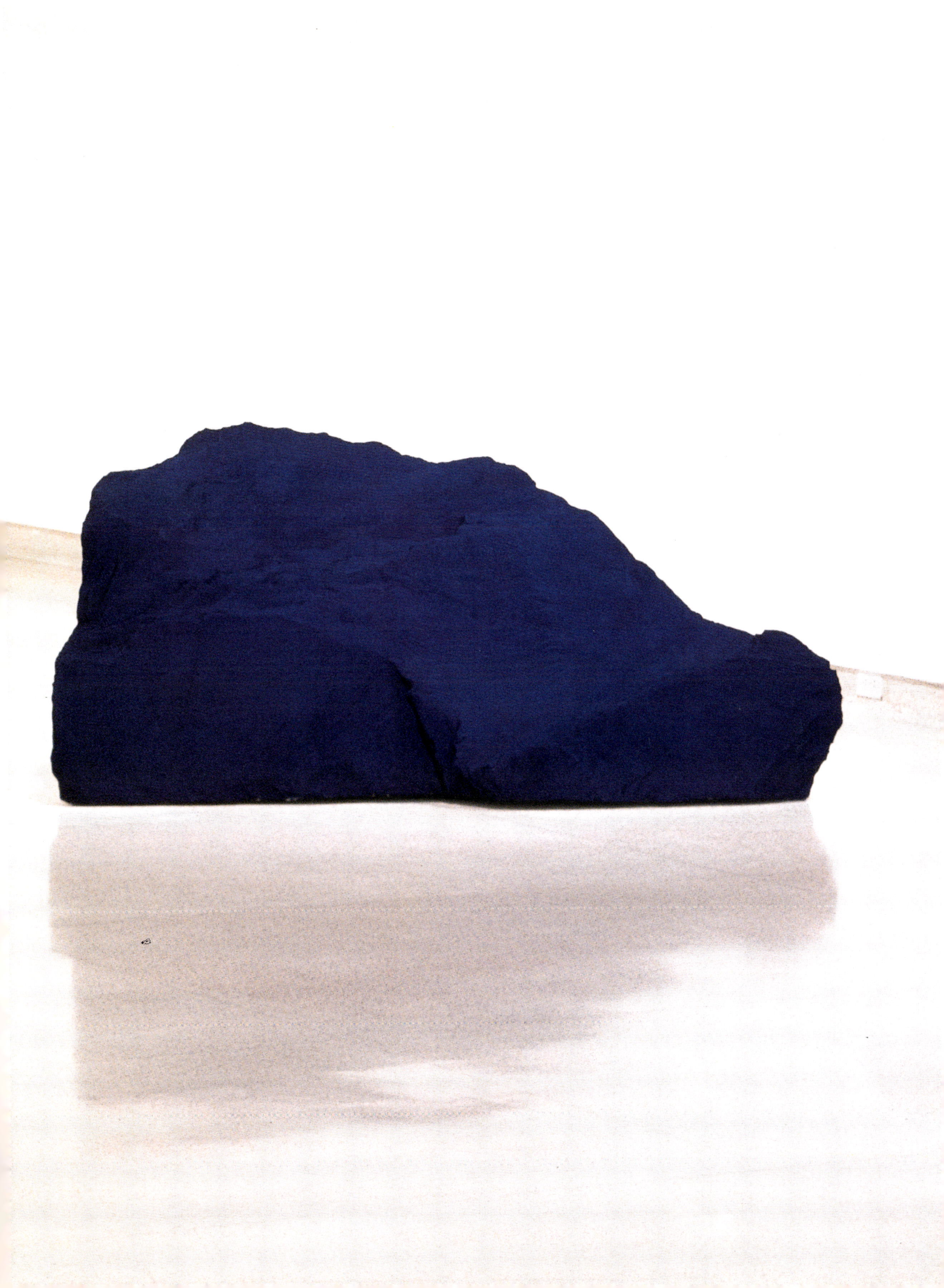

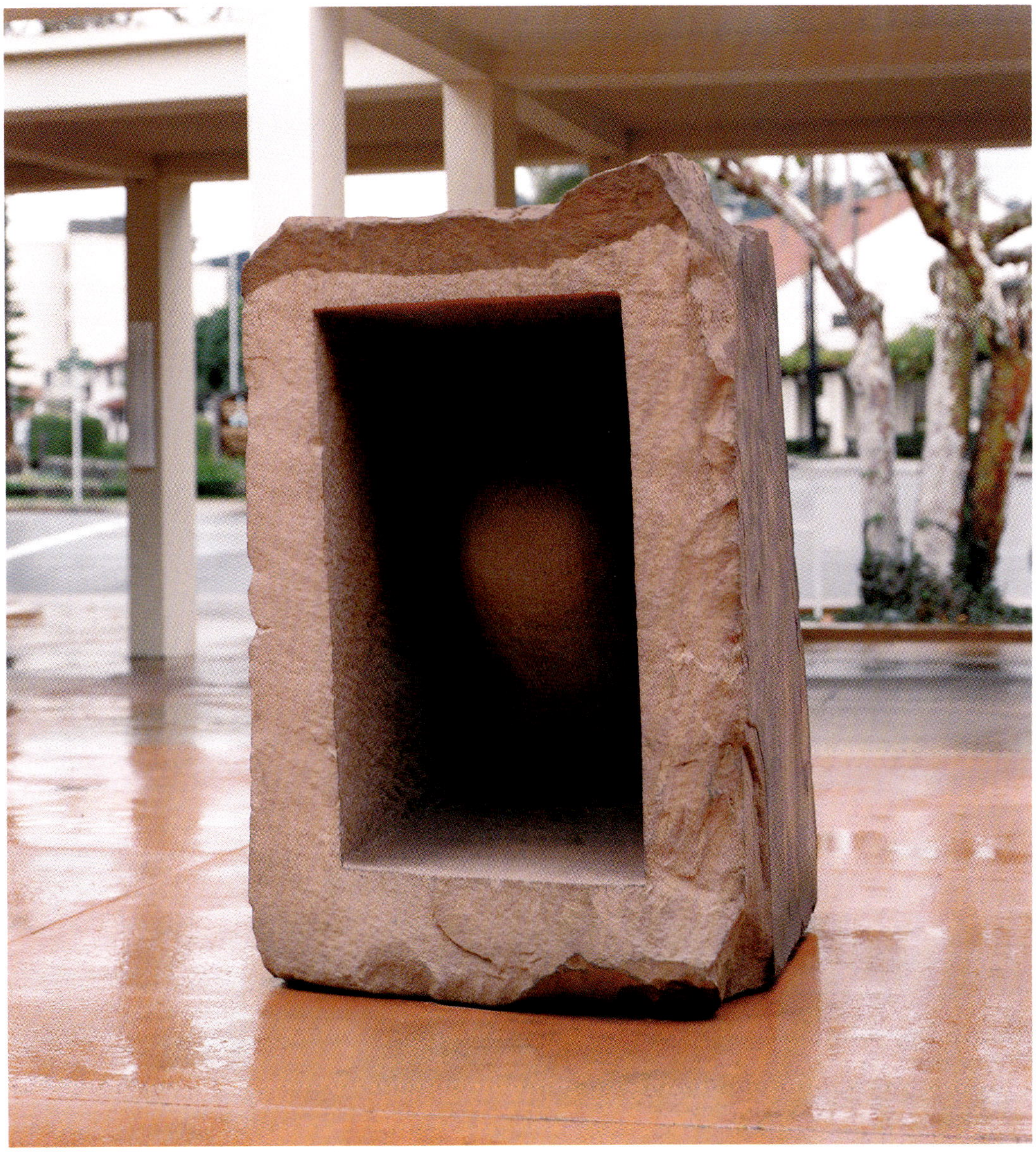

UNTITLED

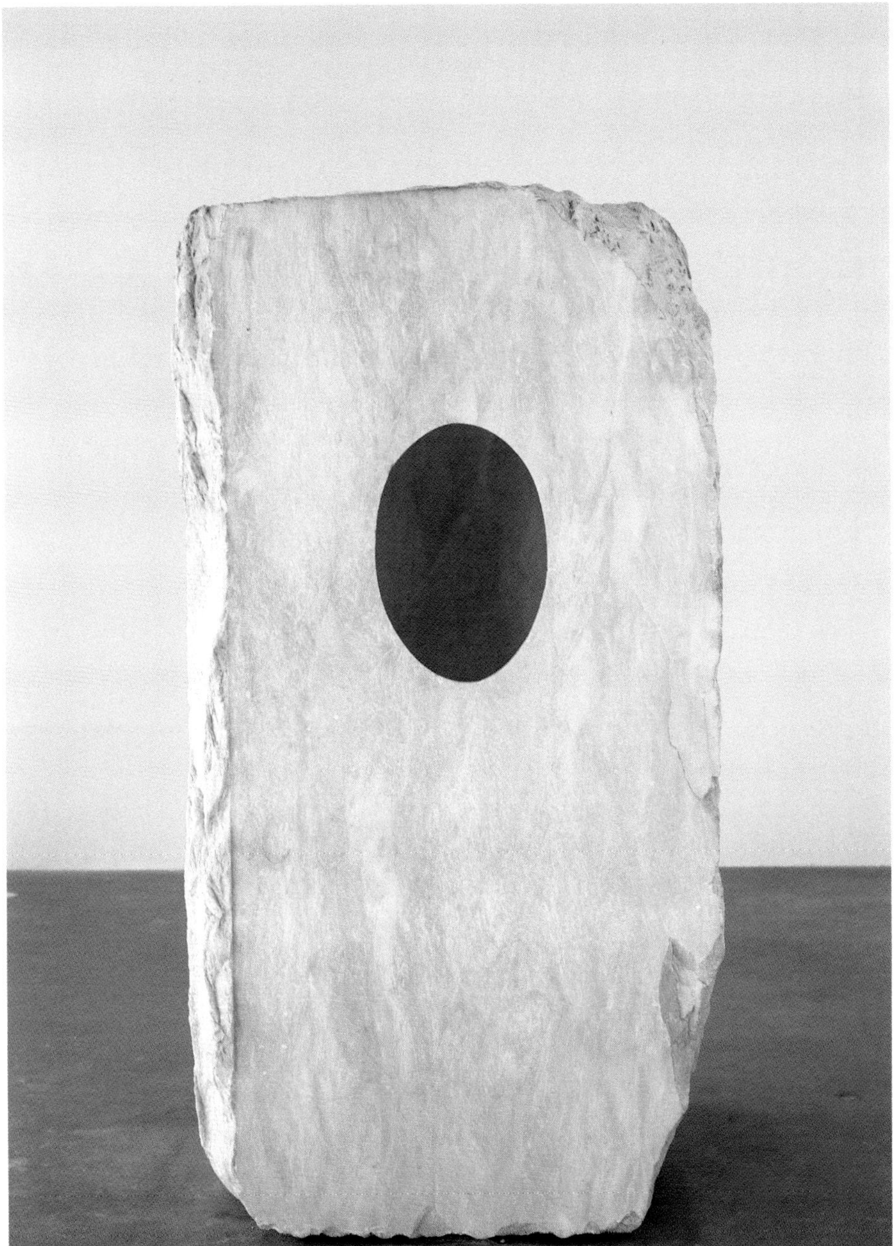

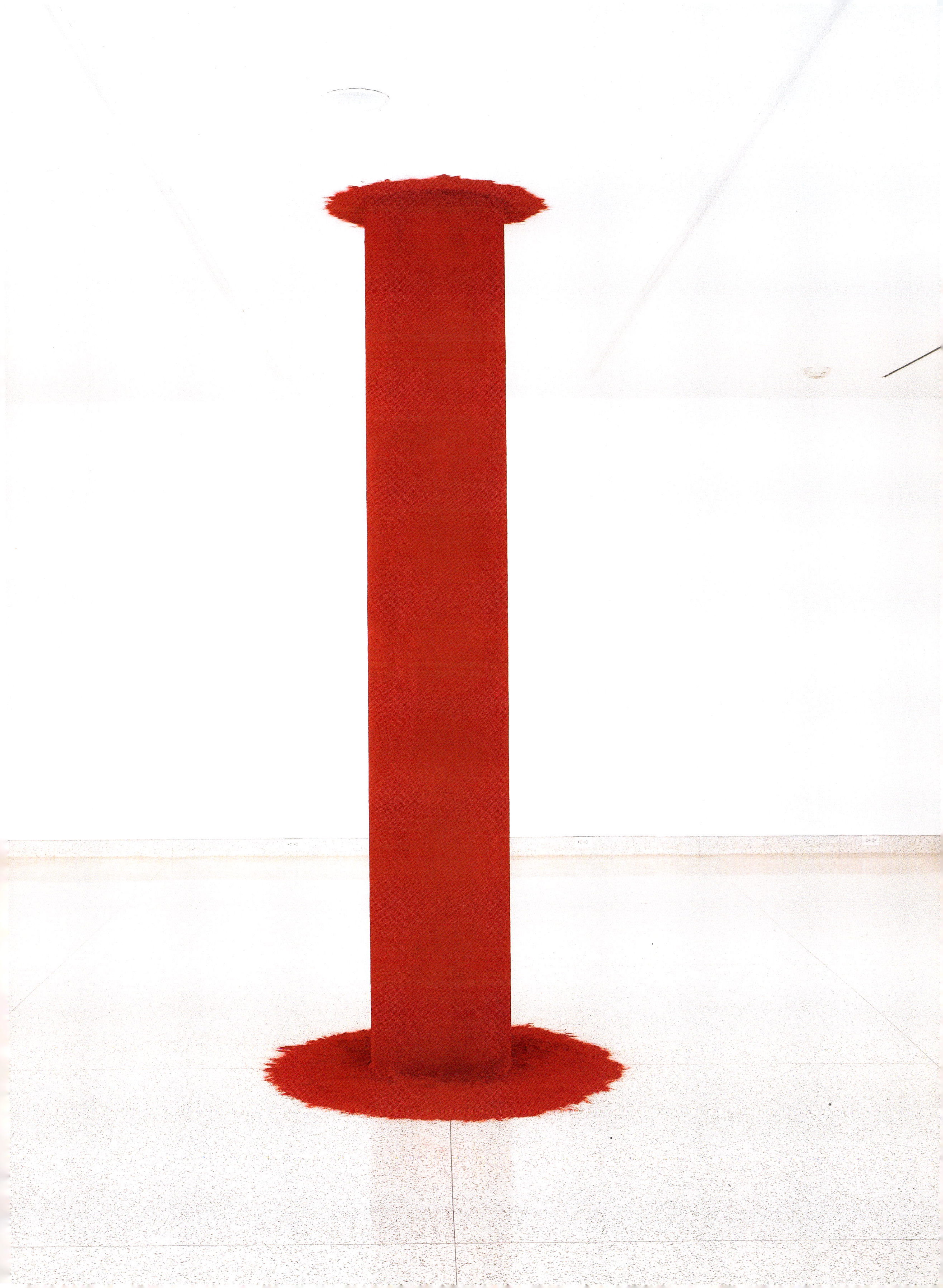

CHECKLIST OF THE EXHIBITION

Height precedes width, width precedes depth.

~ *THE HEALING OF ST. THOMAS*, 1989
mixed media
Museum purchase with funds from the Elizabeth W. Russell Foundation

ANGEL, 1990
slate and pigment
eight parts:
63 1/2" x 64 1/4" x 32 3/4"
31 1/2" x 72" x 33"
16 1/4" x 109 1/2" x 56"
22" x 56" x 42 1/4"
19" x 97" x 65"
26" x 92 1/4" x 51 1/4"
24" x 104" x 44 1/2"
27 1/2" x 107" x 36 1/4"
Courtesy Lisson Gallery, London

UNTITLED, 1990
fiberglas and pigment
three parts: 98 1/2" diameter x 65 3/4" depth each
Courtesy Rijksmuseum Kröller-Müller, Otterlo, Holland; Lisson Gallery, London; and the artist

~ *THE EARTH*, 1991
mixed media
Courtesy the artist

IN THE PRESENCE OF FORM, 1991
sandstone
68" x 45" x 71 1/4"
Courtesy Barbara Gladstone Gallery, New York

PILLAR OF LIGHT, 1991
sandstone
60" x 56 1/2" x 87 1/2"
Courtesy Lisson Gallery, London

UNTITLED, 1991
marble
68 1/2" x 35 1/2" x 36 1/2"
Courtesy Lisson Gallery, London

~ *ENDLESS COLUMN*, 1992
mixed media
Courtesy the artist

~ *WHEN I AM PREGNANT*, 1992
mixed media
Courtesy the artist

~ Installation, dimensions variable

The checklist is as the exhibition appears at the Museum of Contemporary Art, San Diego.
Some works and dimensions will vary at subsequent venues.

BIOGRAPHY

1954	Born, Bombay, India
1973-77	Hornsey College of Art, London, England
1977-78	Chelsea School of Art, London, England
1979	Taught at Wolverhampton Polytechnic, Wolverhampton, England
1982	Artist in Residence, Walker Art Gallery, Liverpool, England
1982-	Lives and works in London, England
1991	Turner Prize Award

ONE-PERSON EXHIBITIONS

1992

Anish Kapoor, Museum of Contemporary Art, San Diego; traveling to the Des Moines Art Center, Des Moines, Iowa; The National Gallery of Canada, Ottawa; The Power Plant, Toronto, Canada

Anish Kapoor, Galeria Soledad Lorenzo, Madrid, Spain

1991

Anish Kapoor, Kunstverein Hannover, Hannover, Germany, organized in cooperation with The British Council

Anish Kapoor, Centro Reina Sofia, Madrid, Spain, organized in cooperation with The British Council

The Sixth Japan Ushimado International Art Festival, Ushimado, Japan

1990-91

Anish Kapoor Drawings, Tate Gallery, London, England

Anish Kapoor, Le Magasin, Centre National d'Art Contemporain, Grenoble, France, organized in cooperation with The British Council

1990

Anish Kapoor, XLIV Biennale di Venezia, British Pavilion, Venice, Italy, organized by The British Council

1989-90

Void Field, Lisson Gallery, London, England

1989

Barbara Gladstone Gallery, New York

Kohji Ogura Gallery, Nagoya, Japan

1988

Lisson Gallery, London, England

1987

Anish Kapoor: Works on Paper 1975-87, Ray Hughes Gallery, Sydney; traveled to Museum of Modern Art, Brisbane, Australia

1986

Anish Kapoor, Kunstnernes Hus, Oslo, Norway

Barbara Gladstone Gallery, New York

Anish Kapoor: Recent Sculpture and Drawings, University Gallery, Fine Arts Center, University of Massachusetts, Amherst, Massachusetts

1985

Lisson Gallery, London, England

Anish Kapoor, Kunsthalle, Basel, Switzerland; traveled to Stedelijk Van Abbemuseum, Eindhoven, The Netherlands

1984

Barbara Gladstone Gallery, New York

1983

Galerie 't Venster, Rotterdam, The Netherlands, organized by the Rotterdam Arts Council

Walker Art Gallery, Liverpool, England; traveled to Le Nouveau Musée, Villeurbanne/Lyon, France

Lisson Gallery, London, England

1982

Lisson Gallery, London, England

Walker Art Gallery, Liverpool, England

1981

Coracle Press, London, England

1980

Patrice Alexandre, Paris, France (studio exhibition)

GROUP EXHIBITIONS

1992

Expo '92, Seville, Spain (in collaboration with David Connor), Documenta 9, Kassel, Germany

1991-92

Rhizome, Haags Gemeentemuseum, The Hague, The Netherlands

1991

Gallery Shirakawa, Kyoto, Japan

Anish Kapoor & Ban Chiang, Feuerle Gallery, Köln, Germany

La Sculpture Contemporaine après 1970, Fondation Daniel Templon, Frejus, France

Trans/Mission, Rooseum, Malmo, Sweden

The 1991 Turner Prize: An Exhibition of Work by the Four Shortlisted Artists, Tate Gallery, London, England

1990-91

British Art Now: A Subjective View, organized by The British Council; traveled to Setagaya Museum, Tokyo; Fukuoka Art Museum; Nagoya City Museum; Tochigi Prefectural Museum of Fine Arts; Hyogo Prefectural Museum; Hiroshima City Museum, Japan

Heroes of Contemporary Art, Galerie Saqqârah, Gstaad, Switzerland; traveled to TransArt Exhibitions, Kreishaus, Köln, Germany

Made of Stone, Galerie Isy Brachot, Brussels, Belgium

1990

Affinities and Intuitions: The Gerald S. Elliott Collection of Contemporary Art, The Art Institute of Chicago, Chicago, Illinois

Dujourie, Fortuyn, Houshiary, Kapoor, Rijksmuseum Kröller-Müller, Otterlo, The Netherlands

Works on Paper, Frith Street Gallery, London, England

1989

Anish Kapoor, Wolfgang Laib, Richard Long, Galerie Le Gall Peyroulet, Paris, France

1988-89

British Now: sculpture et autres dessins, Musée d'art contemporain de Montréal, Montréal, Québec, Canada

Carnegie International, Carnegie Museum of Art, Pittsburgh, Pennsylvania

1988

Britannica: 30 Ans de Sculpture, Musée des Beaux-Arts André Malraux, Le Havre; Ecole d'architecture de Normandie, Darnetal-Rouen; Musée d'Evreux-Anciene Eveche, France

La Couleur Seule, l'Experience du Monochrome, Musée St. Pierre, Lyon, France

Europa oggi / Europe Now, Museo d'Arte Contemporanea, Prato, Italy

Fourth International Drawing Triennale, Kunsthalle Nuremburg, Nuremburg, Germany

Starlit Waters. British Sculpture: An International Art 1968-88, Tate Gallery, Liverpool, England

1987-88

Simila - Dissimila, Kunsthalle, Düsseldorf, Germany; traveled to Columbia University, Sonnabend Gallery, and Leo Castelli Gallery, New York

Viewpoint: L'art contemporain en Grande Bretagne, Musée d'Art Moderne, Brussels, Belgium, organized by The British Council

1987

British Art of the 1980s: 1987, Liljevalchs Konstall, Stockholm, Sweden, organized by The British Council; traveled to Sara Hilden Art Museum, Tampere, Finland

Inside / Outside, Museum Van Hedendaagse Kunst, Antwerpen, Belgium

Juxtapositions: Recent Sculpture from England and Germany, The Institute for Art and Urban Resources, New York

1986

Dessins de Sculpteurs, Galerie Gabrielle Maubrie, Paris, France

Entre el Objeto y la Imagen, Palacio de Velázquez, Madrid, and Fundación Caja de Pensiones, Barcelona, organized by The British Council and Ministerio de Cultura, Spain

General Idea, Anish Kapoor, Melissa Miller, Albright-Knox Art Gallery, Buffalo, New York

Inaugural Exhibition, Lang & O'Hara Gallery, New York

Prospect '86. Eine internationale Austellung aktueller Kunst, Frankfurter Kunstverein, Frankfurt, Germany

Skulptur - 9 Kunstnere fra Storbrittanien, Louisiana Museum of Modern Art, Humlebaek, Denmark

Sonsbeek 1986. International Sculpture Exhibition, Arnhem, The Netherlands

Vessel, Serpentine Gallery, London, England

1985-86

The Poetic Object: Richard Deacon, Shirazeh Houshiary, Anish Kapoor, Douglas Hyde Gallery, Dublin; traveled to the Arts Council Gallery, Belfast, Ireland

1985

7000 Eichen, Kunsthalle, Tübingen; traveled to Kunsthalle, Bielefeld, Germany

20 Sculptures du FRAC Rhone-Alpes, l'Abbaye de Tournus, France

Anish Kapoor and Bill Woodrow, Donald Young Gallery, Chicago, Illinois

Anniottanta, organized by the Cultura del Commune de Ravenna; traveled to Bologna, Imola, Romagna, Italy

The British Show, organized by Art Gallery of New South Wales, Sydney, and The British Council; traveled to Art Gallery of Western Australia, Perth; Art Gallery of New South Wales, Sydney; Queensland Art Gallery, Brisbane; The Exhibition Hall, Melbourne, Australia; National Art Gallery, Wellington, New Zealand

CURRENTS, Institute of Contemporary Art, Boston, Massachusetts

Nouvelle Biennale de Paris, Paris, France

Sculptors' Drawings, organized by the Scottish Arts Council; traveled to Artspace Galleries, Aberdeen; Ayr, Lyth, Stirling, Stromness, Glasgow, Scotland; Dracos Arts Centre, Athens, Greece

Three British Sculptors, Neuberger Museum, State University of New York, Purchase, Purchase, New York

Who's Afraid of Red, Yellow and Blue?, Arnolfini Gallery, Bristol, England

1984

Anish Kapoor and Bill Woodrow, Galerie Paul Maenz, Köln, Germany

The British Art Show: Old Allegiances and New Directions, 1979-1984, organized by the Arts Council of Great Britain; traveled to City of Birmingham Museum and Art Gallery, Birmingham; Ikon Gallery, Birmingham, England; Royal Scottish Academy, Edinburgh, Scotland; Mappin Art Gallery, Sheffield; Southampton Art Gallery, Southampton, England

An International Survey of Recent Painting and Sculpture, The Museum of Modern Art, New York

ROSC '84, Dublin, Ireland

1983

Beelden / Sculpture 1983, Rotterdam Arts Council, Rotterdam, The Netherlands

Constellazione, Galleria Giorgio Persano, Torino, Italy

Douceur de l'Avant-Garde, C'est Rien de le Dire, Rennes, France

Eros Mythos Ironie, Neue Galerie, Graz, Austria

Figures and Objects, John Hansard Gallery, Southampton, England

Finland Biennale, Helsinki, Finland

New Art, Tate Gallery, London, England

Sculpture 1983, Van Krimpen Gallery, Amsterdam, The Netherlands

The Sculpture Show, Hayward Gallery/ Serpentine Gallery, London, England, organized by the Arts Council of Great Britain

Tema Celeste, Museo Civico d'Arte Contemporanea, Gibellina, Italy

Transformations: New Sculpture from Britain, XVII Biennal de São Paulo, Brazil, organized by The British Council; traveled to Museo de Arte Moderna, Rio de Janeiro, Brazil; Museo de Arte Moderna, México, D.F.; Fundacão Calouste Gulbenkien, Lisbon, Portugal

La Trottola di Sirio, Centro d'Arte Contemporanea, Siracusa, Italy, organized by The British Council

1982

Aperto '82, XL Biennale di Venezia, Venice, Italy

Englische Plastik Heute/British Sculpture Now, Kunstmuseum, Luzern, Switzerland

India: Myth and Reality, Museum of Modern Art, Oxford, England

London/New York 1982, Lisson Gallery, London, England

Objects and Figures: New Sculpture in Britain, Fruitmarket Gallery, Edinburgh, Scotland, organized by the Scottish Arts Council

Paris Biennale, Paris, France

Prefiguration, Centre d'Art Contemporain, Chambéry, France

1981

British Sculpture in the 20th Century, Part Two: Symbol and Imagination 1951-80, Whitechapel Art Gallery, London, England

Objects & Sculpture: Richard Deacon, Antony Gormley, Anish Kapoor, Peter Randall-Page, Institute of Contemporary Art, London; traveled to Arnolfini Gallery, Bristol, England

Summer Show, Serpentine Gallery, London, England

1980

New Sculpture, Midland Group Gallery, Nottingham, England

1979

Tolly Cobbold: Eastern Arts, 2nd National Exhibition, Fitzwilliam Museum, Cambridge, England; traveling exhibition

1978

Northern Young Contemporaries, Whitworth Art Gallery, Manchester, England

1975

Young Contemporaries, Royal Academy of Art, London, England

1974

Art into Landscape 1, Serpentine Gallery, London, England

SELECTED BIBLIOGRAPHY

1992

Anish Kapoor. Exhibition catalogue; introduction by Lynda Forsha and essay by Pier Luigi Tazzi. La Jolla, California: Museum of Contemporary Art, San Diego.

"Journey to the centre of a void." *The Independent*, London, January 8.

Assisi, Francis. "Music of Begum Akhtar Has Enduring Appeal." *India West*, San Francisco, March 13, 56.

Baker, Kenneth. "Between a Rock and a Soft Place." *San Francisco Chronicle*, February 26.

Bevan, Roger. "Anish Kapoor wins Turner Prize." *The Art Newspaper*, London, January14.

Clothier, Peter. "Metaphor or Metaphysics: Jackie Winsor and Anish Kapoor." *Artspace*, May-June, 44-49.

Freudenheim, Susan. "Creating Art from a Diverse Heritage." *Los Angeles Times*, January 31, F1, F10.

Jarmusch, Ann. "Dark and Dangerous: Kapoor sculpture mystical, alluring." *San Diego Tribune*, January 31, C1, C6.

Keller, Sue. "Anish Kapoor: making sculpture un-three dimensional." *La Jolla Light*, February 13, C1, C5.

Knight, Christopher. "Painterly Sculptures, Illusion by Kapoor." *Los Angeles Times*, February 5, F8.

Lister, Priscilla. "Anish Kapoor: Contradictions Say Something." *San Diego Daily Transcript*, January 29, 1A, 6A.

Pincus, Robert L. "Kapoor's fame far exceeds his ego." *The San Diego Union-Tribune*, February 2.

________. "Sublime case of the blues." *Night and Day/San Diego Union-Tribune*, March 5, 36.

1991

Anish Kapoor. Exhibition catalogue; essay by Eckhard Schneider. Hannover, Germany: Kunstverein Hannover.

Anish Kapoor. Exhibition catalogue; Spanish edition of XLIV Biennalle di Venezia catalogue. Madrid: Centro de Arte Reina Sofia and The British Council.

Anish Kapoor & Ban Chiang. Exhibition catalogue; essay by Angel Garcia. Köln: Feuerle Gallery.

"Hacia el esplendor." *El Pais*, Madrid, February 17, 4-5.

La Sculpture Contemporaine après 1970. Exhibition catalogue. Frejus, France: Fondation Daniel Templon.

"Lupertz y Kapoor, dos voces europeas de los ochenta." *ABC*, Madrid, February 14, 126.

"A Prize Turnabout." *Daily Telegraph*, London, July 16.

"El Reina Sofia, en plena actividad." *El Punto*, Madrid, February 12, 18.

Trans/Mission. Exhibition catalogue. Malmo, Sweden: Rooseum.

The Turner Prize 1991. Exhibition catalogue; essay by Sean Rainbird. London: Tate Gallery.

"Turner Prize for Anish Kapoor." *Indian Weekly*, London, December.

Allthorpe-Guyton, Marjorie. "Made in Heaven." *Artscribe* (December): 15.

Baker, Kenneth. "Sculptures Go Two-Dimensional." *San Francisco Chronicle*, February 20.

Bierens, Cornel. "Urformen der Kulturen." *Kolner Stadtanzeiger (KSTA)*, Köln, March 21.

Borras, Maria Luisa. "Anish Kapoor exhibe esculturas de origine cromatismo en el Palacio Velázquez." *La Vanguardia*, Madrid, February 18, 35.

de Baranano, Kosme Maria. "Anish Kapoor." *Lapiz*, Madrid (June): 28-35.

de Bustos, C. I. "Torres, Lupertz, Brossa y Kapoor: cita de la ultimas tendencias en el CARSS." *ABC*, Madrid, February 5, 50.

Dorment, Richard. "A Winner in a class of his own." *Daily Telegraph*, London, November 27.

Eickhoff, Beate. "Anish Kapoor und GefaBe der Ban-Chiang-Kultur." *Kunstforum* (May/June): 365-6.

Gale, Iain and Dalya Alberge. "Youth and beauty?" *The Independent*, London, July 16.

Galligan, Gregory. "Steamed-Up Mirrors and Boogie-Woogies." *Art International*, Paris (Spring/Summer): 14.

Ikoma, Yoshiko. "Anish Kapoor: Interview." *Crea*, Japan, No. 5, 152-53.

Kent, Sarah. "Prize Fighters." *Time Out*, London (November).

Llorca, Pablo. "Literatura complicada, obra sencilla." *Diario 16*, Madrid, March 8, 42.

Lubbock, Tom. "Shortlist short on ideas." *The Independent*, London, July 21.

Mon, Jose. "Anish Kapoor, la escultura y el presente." *El Punto*, Madrid, March 8.

Morgan, Stuart. "The Turner Prize." *Frieze* (October): 4-8.

Overy, Paul. "Lions and Unicorns: The Britishness of Postwar British Sculpture." *Art in America* (September): 104-11.

Piguet, Philippe. "Monolithes et Monochromes." *La Croix*, France, January 15.

Picazo, Gloria. "Anish Kapoor." *Lapiz*, Madrid (February).

Plimmer, Martin. "Searching for the art of the matter." *London Standard*, London, November 6.

Steevensz, Bert. "Anish Kapoor." *Metropolis M*, Utrecht (February): 48.

Torres, Lupertz. "Kapoor y Brossa, en el Reina." *El Punto*, Madrid, February 14,19.

Touraine, Liliane. "Anish Kapoor, De la modification pour principe a un symbolisme de l'universal." *Artefactum* (April/May): 9-11.

1990

"XLIV Venice Biennale 1990." *Visual Arts News*, The British Council (January): 1.

Affinities and Intuitions: The Gerald S. Elliott Collection of Contemporary Art. Exhibition catalogue; Neal Benezra (ed.). Chicago: The Art Institute of Chicago and Thames and Hudson.

Anish Kapoor: British Pavilion, XLIV Venice Biennale. Exhibition catalogue; essay by Thomas McEvilley and interview by Marjorie Allthorpe-Guyton. London: The British Council.

Anish Kapoor: Drawings. Exhibition catalogue; essay by Jeremy Lewison. London: Tate Gallery Publications.

"Anish Kapoor interviewed by Douglas Maxwell." *Art Monthly* (May): 6-12.

Blau: Farbe der Ferne. Hans Gercke (ed.). Wunderhorn, Heidelberg.

British Art Now: A Subjective View. Exhibition catalogue; essays by Akio Obigane and Junichi Shioda. Japan: Asahi Shimbun and The British Council.

Dujourie, Fortuyn, Houshiary, Kapoor. Exhibition catalogue; essay by Marianne Brouwer. Otterlo: Rijksmuseum Kröller-Müller.

Heroes of Contemporary Art. Exhibition catalogue; essays by Akim Monet. Gstaad, Switzerland: Galerie Saqqârah.

Surrogaat/Surrogate: 15 years of Galerie 't Venster from Kiefer to Koons. Jan Donia (ed.). SDU Uitgeverij, Amstelveen.

Allthorpe-Guyton, Marjorie. "Anish Kapoor: Lisson Gallery." *Artforum* (March): 175-76.

________. "Original Sites: The Sculpture of Anish Kapoor." *Artscribe* (May): 50-52.

Archer, Michael. "No solo Escultura: Inglaterre." *Lapiz*, Madrid (Summer): 44-48.

Buck, Louisa. "Pigments of the Imagination." *Sunday Correspondent*, London, May 13, 10-14.

Curtis, Penelope. "Sculpture on the Threshold." *The Antique Collector* (May): 66-73.

Feaver, William. "Venice, vidi, vici: William Feaver at the Biennale." *Vogue* (May): 68

________. "Anish Kapoor: Lisson Gallery." *ARTnews* (April): 179.

Garlake, Margaret. "Brown bagging in Venice." *Art Monthly* (July): 3-5.

Graham-Dixon, Andrew. "Venice Biennale 1990." *Audio Arts Magazine*, vol. 10, no. 4.

Hindry, Ann. "Champs de pierre d'Anish Kapoor." *Beaux Arts* (June): 64-77.

Kent, Sarah. "Mind Over Matter." *20/20* (May): 36-40.

Kimmelman, Michael. "Venice Biennale Opens With Surprises." *The New York Times*, May 28, C11, C14.

Mays, John Bentley. "Looking at the inwardness of things." *The Globe and Mail*, London, May 30, C7.

Obigane, Akio. "Anish Kapoor." *Atelier* (January): 2-24.

Pejic, Bojana. "What will become of our sensitive skin...." *Artforum* (September): 130-32.

Plagens, Peter. "Venetian Carnival." *Newsweek*, June 11, 60-61.

Renton, Andrew. "Anish Kapoor: Lisson." *Flash Art* (March-April): 151-52.

Smulders, Caroline. "Anish Kapoor: Vers la dematerialisation de l'object." (interview) *art press* (November): 16-21.

Van Drateln, Doris. "Anish Kapoor: Ein Gesprach." *Kunstforum* (August/October): 304-14.

Watkins, Jonathan. "Venice Biennale Preview: Anish Kapoor." *Art International* (Summer): 86.

1989

Anish Kapoor. Exhibition catalogue; essay by Pier Luigi Tazzi. Nagoya, Japan: Kohji Ogura Gallery, in cooperation with Lisson Gallery, London.

Auty, Giles. "Anish Kapoor at Lisson Gallery." *Spectator*, London, December 16, 35.

Cork, Richard. "Airy as a Rock." *Listener*, London, December 14, 42.

Currah, Mark. "Anish Kapoor: Lisson Gallery." *City Limits*, London, December 21, 109.

Dectur, Joshua. "New York in Review." *Arts Magazine* (September): 92-105.

Dorment, Richard. "Vexed questions of colour." *Daily Telegraph*, London, December 9.

Feaver, William. "Voices from the void." *Observer*, London, December 10, 44.

Graham-Dixon, Andrew. "Pride and Prejudice." *The Independent*, London, December 5.

Kapoor, Anish, Sylvie Primard, and Pier Luigi Tazzi. "Mother as a Mountain." *Artforum* (September): 126-31.

Kent, Sarah. "Anish Kapoor." *Time Out*, London, December 13.

Lillington, David. "Anish Kapoor: Lisson Gallery." *Arts Review*, December 15, 889-90.

Meer, Ameena. "Anish Kapoor." *BOMB* (Winter): 38-43.

Packer, William. "Sculptor with the best of both worlds." *Financial Times*, London, December 12.

Princenthal, Nancy. "Anish Kapoor at Barbara Gladstone." *Art in America* (October): 217.

Schjeldahl, Peter. "Earthy but House-broken." *7 Days*, New York, April 19.

Vaizey, Marina. "Why partiality does not tell the whole story." *Sunday Times*, London, December 10.

Westfall, Stephen. "Anish Kapoor: Barbara Gladstone Gallery." *Flash Art* (Summer): 147.

1988

Britannica: 30 Ans de Sculpture. Exhibition catalogue; essays by Catherine Grenier, Françoise Cohen, and Lynne Cooke. Le Havre: Musée des Beaux Arts André Malraux, Le Musée d'Evreaux-Anciene Eveche, L'Ecole d' Architecture de Normandie, Darnetal-Rouen.

British Now: sculpture et autres dessins. Exhibition catalogue; essay by Sandra Grant Marchand. Montréal, Canada: Musée d'art contemporain de Montréal.

Carnegie International. Exhibition catalogue; essays by John Caldwell, Vicky A. Clark, Thomas McEvilley, Lynne Cooke, and Milena Kalinovska. Pittsburgh, Pennsylvania: The Carnegie Museum of Art.

La Couleur seule, l'Experience du Monochrome. Exhibition catalogue. Lyon, France: Musée St. Pierre.

Europa oggi/Europe now. Exhibition catalogue; Amnon Barzel (ed.). Prato, Italy: Museo d'Arte Contemporanea.

Fourth International Drawing Triennale. Exhibition catalogue; essay by David Reason. Nuremburg: Kunsthalle Nuremburg.

Starlit Waters. British Sculpture: An International Art 1968-88. Exhibition catalogue; essays by Martin Kunz, Charles Harrison, and Lynne Cooke. Liverpool: Tate Gallery.

Kent, Sarah. "Anish Kapoor at Lisson." *Art in America* (September): 201.

Lee, David. "Anish Kapoor: Lisson Gallery." *Arts Review*, April 22, 269-70.

Martin, Rupert. "Anish Kapoor: The Journey from an Earthly to a Heavenly Body." *Flash Art* (Summer): 159.

Vaizey, Marina. "Shaping up to Abstracts." *Sunday Times*, London.

1987-88

Simila - Dissimila. Exhibition catalogue; Rainer Crone (ed.), text by Cornelia Lauf. Düsseldorf: Kunsthalle.

Viewpoint: L'art contemporain en Grande Bretagne. Exhibition catalogue; interview by Richard Cork. The British Council and Museum of Modern Art, Brussels.

1987

Anish Kapoor: Works on Paper 1975-1987. Exhibition catalogue; interview by Richard Cork. Brisbane: Ray Hughes Gallery.

British Art of the 1980s. Exhibition catalogue; text by Lynne Cooke. The British Council.

Inside/Outside: An Aspect of Contemporary Art. Exhibition catalogue; essay by Jan Fonce. Antwerpen: Museum Van Hedendaagse Kunst.

Juxtapositions: Recent Sculpture from England and Germany. Exhibition catalogue. New York: The Institute for Art and Urban Resources.

A Quiet Revolution: British Sculpture Since 1965. Exhibition catalogue; essays by Graham Beal, Lynne Cooke, Mary Jane Jacob, and Alan Nawrocki. Chicago: Museum of Contemporary Art and San Francisco Museum of Modern Art.

Bonaventura, Paul. "An Introduction to Recent British Sculpture." *Artefactum* (September-October).

1986

Anish Kapoor. Exhibition catalogue; texts by Arne Malmedal and Lynne Cooke. Oslo: Kunstnernes Hus.

Anish Kapoor. Exhibition brochure; essay by Helen Raye. Buffalo, New York: Albright-Knox Art Gallery.

Anish Kapoor: Recent Sculpture and Drawings. Exhibition catalogue; text by Helaine Posner. Amherst: University Gallery, Fine Arts Center, University of Massachusetts.

Entre el Objeto y la Imagen. Exhibition catalogue; texts by Lewis Biggs and Juan Muñoz. The British Council and Ministerio de Cultura, Spain.

Prospect '86. Eine interenationale Austellung aktueller Kunst. Exhibition catalogue. Frankfurt, Germany: Frankfurter Kunstverein.

Skulptur - 9 Kunstnere fra Storbrittanien. Exhibition catalogue; essays by Oystein Hjort and Lynne Cooke. Humlebaek, Denmark: Louisiana Museum of Modern Art.

Sonsbeek 1986. International Sculpture Exhibition. Exhibition catalogue. Arnhem, The Netherlands.

Kuspit, Donald. "Anish Kapoor: Barbara Gladstone." *Artforum* (November): 129-30.

Russell, John. "Bright Young Talents: Six Artists with a Future." *The New York Times*, May 18, Section 2, 1, 31.

1985

7000 Eichen. Exhibition catalogue; essay by Heiner Bastian. Tübingen, Germany: Kunsthalle, Tübingen.

Anish Kapoor. Exhibition catalogue; texts by Jean-Christophe Ammann, Alexander von Grevenstein, and Ananda Coomaraswamy. Basel, Switzerland: Kunsthalle, Basel.

The British Show. Exhibition catalogue; text by Stuart Morgan. Sydney, Australia: Art Gallery of New South Wales.

CURRENTS. Exhibition catalogue; text by David Joselit. Boston, Massachusetts: The Institute of Contemporary Art.

"Neues aus Amerika und Indien." *Der Bund*, Bern, October 10.

"Noli me tangere und Beruhren gestattet." *Basellandschaftliche Zeitung*, Liestal (Switzerland), October 9.

La Nouvelle Biennale de Paris. Exhibition catalogue. Paris: Musée national d'art moderne, Centre Georges Pompidou.

The Poetic Object: Richard Deacon, Shirazeh Houshiary, Anish Kapoor. Exhibition catalogue; text by Richard Francis. Dublin: Douglas Hyde Gallery.

"A text by Anish Kapoor." *Lo Spazio Umano* (July-September): 77.

Arnold, Bruce. "Close look at new British sculpture." *The Independent*, London, November 24.

Bohm-Duchen, Monica. "Anish Kapoor: Lisson." *Flash Art* (December-January): 49.

Collier, Caroline. "Forms a hole can take...: Anish Kapoor, Lisson Gallery, London." *Studio International*, 43-44.

Gassert, Siegmar. "Tisch und Stuhl und Kreis und Kugel und Muschel." *Basler Zeitung*, Basel, October 7.

Hollenstein, Roman. "Von Johns und Artschwager bis Kapoor." *Neue Zurcher Zeitung*, Zurich, October 10.

Kent, Sarah. "Review." *Time Out*, London, September 19-25.

Mathonnet, Philippe. "Poudre aux yeux et faux bois!" *Journal de Geneve*, Geneva, October 19.

Packer, William. "The age of discardment." *Financial Times*, London, September 19.

Paparoni, Demetrio. "Spazio di Dio, spazio della Terra." *Tema Celeste*, Siracusa, 46-49.

Vaizey, Marina. "A new star carves out a sculpture for our time." *Sunday Times*, London, September 8.

Vedrenne, Elisabeth. "L'illusion du desir." *Decoration Internationale*, Paris (October): 41-44.

Zwez, Anneliese. "Zwei Pole: Intellektuelle Konzepte und sinnliche Strahlkraft." *Aargauer Tagblatt*, Switzerland, October 17.

1984

"Anish Kapoor." *Arts Magazine* (May): 44.

The British Art Show: Old Allegiances and New Directions, 1979-1984. Exhibition catalogue; texts by Jon Thompson, Alexander Moffat, and Marjorie Allthorpe-Guyton. The Arts Council of Great Britain.

An International Survey of Recent Painting and Sculpture. Exhibition catalogue; introduction by Kynaston McShine. New York: The Museum of Modern Art.

ROSC '84. Exhibition catalogue. Dublin, Ireland.

"Sculptor Anish Kapoor." *Art Gallery* (December-January): 33.

Baker, Kenneth. "Anish Kapoor at Barbara Gladstone." *Art in America* (October): 189-90.

Cameron, Dan. "Anish Kapoor." *Arts Magazine* (March): 4.

Coleman, John. "Anish Kapoor: Lisson Gallery." *Flash Art* (January): 39.

Handy, Ellen. "Anish Kapoor." *Arts Magazine* (May): 44.

Newman, Michael. "Discourse and Desire: Recent British Sculpture." *Flash Art* (January): 48-55.

Princenthal, Nancy. "Anish Kapoor." *ARTnews* (Summer): 189.

Russell, John Taylor. "Anish Kapoor." *The New York Times*, March 23, Weekend Section.

________. "Art: Inaugural Show Is Survey of New Work." *The New York Times*, May 18.

1983

Anish Kapoor: Beeldhouwwerken. Exhibition catalogue; text by Michael Newman. Organized by Rotterdam Arts Council; Galerie 't Venster, Rotterdam.

"Anish Kapoor. Bombay, Londra." *Domus* (February): 69.

Beelden / Sculpture 1983. Exhibition catalogue; Gosse and Cees Van der Geer (eds.); text by Oosterhaf, with essay by Paul Hefting. Rotterdam Arts Council.

Douceur de l'Avant-Garde. Exhibition catalogue. Rennes, France: C'est Rien de le Dire.

Feeling into Form. Exhibition catalogue; text by Marco Livingstone. Liverpool: Walker Art Gallery and Le Nouveau Musée, Lyon.

Figures and Objects: Recent Developments in British Sculpture. Exhibition catalogue; essay by Michael Newman. Southampton, England: John Hansard Gallery, The University, Southampton.

Hayward Annual. Exhibition catalogue; text by Stuart Morgan talking with Kate Blacker. London: Hayward Gallery, South Bank Centre.

New Art. Exhibition catalogue; essay by Michael Compton. London: Tate Gallery.

The Sculpture Show. Exhibition catalogue; essays by Kate Blacker, Fenella Crichton, Paul de Monchaux, Nena Dimitrijevic, Stuart Morgan, Deanna Petherbridge, Bryan Robertson, and Nicholas Wadley. The Arts Council of Great Britain.

Tema Celeste. Exhibition catalogue; text by Demetrio Paparoni. Gibellina: Museo Civico d'Arte Contemporanea.

Transformations: New Sculpture from Britain. Exhibition catalogue for XVII Bienal de São Paulo; introduction by Nicholas Serota, essays by Lewis Biggs, Lynne Cooke, Mark Francis, John McEwen, Stuart Morgan, and John Roberts. London: The British Council.

La Trottola di Sirio. Exhibition catalogue; text by Demetrio Paparoni. Organized by The British Council. Siracusa: Centro d'Arte Contemporanea.

Baillieu, Amanda. "Strange Monoliths." *LAM Magazine* (October).

Beaumont, Mary Rose. "Anish Kapoor: Lisson Gallery." *Arts Review*, October 28, 622.

________. "Anish Kapoor, Lisson Gallery." *Arts Review*, November 11.

________. "The Sculpture Show." *Arts Review*, September.

Castello, Michaelangelo. "Se il vero prende corpo." *Tema Celeste* (November): 12-15.

Collier, Caroline. "Anish Kapoor at the Lisson Gallery." *Studio International* (December): 51.

Cork, Richard. "Lucid Form." *London Standard*, London, November 3.

Dutt, Robin. "Anish Kapoor." *New Life*, November 18.

Groot, Paul. "Anish Kapoor: 't Venster Gallery." *Flash Art* (May): 70-71.

Januszczak, Waldemar. "Three into two won't go." *Guardian*, London, August 16.

Kent, Sarah. "Review." *Time Out*, London, November 3-9.

Kinmouth, Patrick. "Anish Kapoor's Shades of Meaning." *Vogue* (August): 104-7.

Lucie-Smith, Edward. "Back in touch with the emotions." *Sunday Times*, London, August 21.

Newman, Michael. "Le drame du desir dans la sculpture d'Anish Kapoor." *Art Press* (May): 31-33.

________. "Figuren und Objekte: Neue Skulptur in England." *Kunstforum* (June): 22-35.

Paparoni, Demetrio. "Le radici della forma." *Tema Celeste* (November): 4-9.

Taylor, John Russell. "Playing into the hands of those who pour scorn." *Sunday Times*, London, August 16.

1982

XL Biennale di Venezia. Exhibition catalogue; text for "Aperto '82" by Tommaso Trini.

British Sculpture Now: Tony Cragg, Stephen Cox, Richard Deacon, Anish Kapoor, Bill Woodrow. Exhibition catalogue; introduction by Martin Kunz (ed.), essays by Flavio Caroli, Fabrizio D'Amico, and Michael Newman. Lucerne, Switzerland: Kunstmuseum Luzern.

Objects and Figures: New Sculpture in Britain. Exhibition catalogue. The Scottish Arts Council.

Collier, Caroline. "Anish Kapoor." *Arts Review*, June 4, 289-90.

Feaver, William. "Gaz Mask." *ARTnews* (September): 123.

McEwan, John. *The Spectator*, London, June.

Newman, Michael. "Anish Kapoor." *Art Monthly* (July-August): 15.

________. "New Sculpture in Britain." *Art in America* (September): 104-14, 177, 179.

Vaizey, Marina. "Anish Kapoor." *Sunday Times*, London, May.

1981

British Sculpture in the Twentieth Century, Part Two: Symbol and Imagination 1951-80. Exhibition catalogue; Sandy Nairne and Nicholas Serota (eds.), essay by Stuart Morgan. London: Whitechapel Art Gallery.

Objects and Sculpture. Exhibition catalogue; texts by Lewis Biggs, Owona Blazwick, and Sandy Nairne. London: Institute of Contemporary Art and Arnolfini Gallery, Bristol.

Feaver, William. "An Air of Light Relief." *Observer*, London, June 26.

STAFF

ADMINISTRATION
Hugh M. Davies, *Director*
Charles E. Castle, *Associate Director/ Finance & Administration*
Linda Taylor Fonte, *Accounting Manager*
Michelle Hautau, *Assistant to the Director*
Suzannah Banet, *Accounting Assistant*
DeAnn Long, Receptionist

CURATORIAL
Lynda Forsha, *Curator*
Madeleine Grynsztejn, *Associate Curator*
Mary Johnson, *Registrar*
Nerissa Dominguez, *Curatorial Assistant*
Dennis Sopczynski, *Graphic Designer* *
Erika Torri, *Librarian* *
Juanita Purner, *NEA Dos Ciudades/Two Cities Fellow*
William Bulkley, *Preparator*

DEVELOPMENT
Anne Farrell, *Development Director*
Diane Maxwell, *Public Relations Officer*
Gretchen Davison, *Membership Coordinator*
Debra Palmer, *Development Assistant*
Cheryl Butler Lee, *Special Events Coordinator* *
Eleanor Winans, *Volunteer Coordinator* *
Debra Achen, *Public Relations Assistant* *

50th ANNIVERSARY CAMPAIGN
Liza Boyer, *Campaign Director*
Lisa Morrow, *Campaign Assistant*

FACILITY & SECURITY
Tom Flowers, *Museum Manager*
Matthew Clowminzer, *Maintenance*
Tauno Hannula, *Gardener*
Terrence Overson, *Chief of Security*
Lauren Griffin, *Museum Attendant* *
Marion Knight, *Museum Attendant* *
David Lowry, *Museum Attendant*
Ken Maloney, *Museum Attendant*
Lily Sanchez, *Museum Attendant* *
Kaled Zakriya, *Museum Attendant* *

SHERWOOD AUDITORIUM
Gwen Fowler, *Business Manager*
Chris Overson, *Production Manager*
Spencer Combs, *Events Manager* *
Michael Scheer, *Events Manager**
Thomas Stansell, *Events Manager* *

BOOKSTORE
Joan Dalrymple, *Bookstore Manager*
Catherine Gleason, *Bookstore Clerk* *
Carol Kinter, *Bookstore Clerk* *
Al Margraff, *Bookstore Clerk* *
Karen Smith, *Bookstore Clerk* *

** Denotes Part Time*

Design ~ *Dennis J. Sopczynski*
Compositor ~ *Eric Gill, Perpetua*
Photography ~ *Philipp Scholz Rittermann*
System ~ *Macintosh IIcx / Pagemaker 4.01*
Linotronic Output ~ *Central Graphics, San Diego*
Printing ~ *Rush Press, San Diego*